On the Sunny Side

On the Sunny Side

The Danbury Mad Hatter Chorus 1966–2016

Wynn Gadkar-Wilcox

Danbury, Connecticut, The Mad Hatter Chorus, 2017

Library of Congress Control Number: 2017916732
International Standard Book Number 978-0-6929732-1-9

© 2017 by the Mad Hatter Chorus
All rights reserved

Cover Photo: Gordon Finch of Bethel, CT, sings with the Mad Hatters at the Swampfield Soiree in June 1985. Photo provided courtesy of Gordon Finch and the *News-Times*.

Distributed by the Mad Hatter Chorus
104 Lexington Blvd.
Bethel, CT 06801

Printed in U.S.A.

Contents

List of Figures vi

Acknowledgements ix

1 No Message, Just Pleasure
   The Early Years, 1966–1973 1

2 "More Schmaltz"
   The Golden Years of Tony Grosz and Ray Wixted,
   1973–1987 29

3 "Maintaining the Tonal Center"
   Struggling for Existence in a Changing World,
   1987–2002 73

4 "The Danbury Sound"
   The Era of the Young Directors, 2002–2016 91

Epilogue 111

Selected Bibliography 117

Index 121

List of Figures

Figure 1.1	Charter Night Flyer	5
Figure 1.2	Receiving the Charter	7
Figure 1.3	The Persuaders performing in 1966	8
Figure 1.4	The Nutmeggers	13
Figure 1.5	Program Cover of the 1971 Annual Show	16
Figure 1.6	Bill Manion directing the Mad Hatter Chorus in 1971	18
Figure 1.7	The Mad Hatters performing on their 1971 Annual Show	19
Figure 1.8	The Lavender Hill Mob	20
Figure 1.9	Sweater patch of the Mad Hatter Chorus, designed by illustrator Frank Golden	23
Figure 2.1	Fifth place ribbons from the District Contest, 1977 and 1981	31
Figure 2.2	The Mad Hatter Chorus at the District Competition in Lake Placid, NY, October 1973	33
Figure 2.3	Last Call	36
Figure 2.4	The Brotherhood at the 1977 International Convention	38
Figure 2.5	Preparing makeup for the 1977 District Contest	47
Figure 2.6	Final Decision	50
Figure 2.7	Chorus President Bob Smith pins the Director's Award on Director Ray Wixted, District Contest, 1981	55

Figure 2.8	Summertime	57
Figure 2.9	Bob Connolley enjoying the annual clambake, 1978	58
Figure 2.10	Sterling Edition	64
Figure 3.1	The Connecticut Wailers	80
Figure 3.3	The Mad Hatters at the Division Contest, Norwich, CT, April 1990	82
Figure 3.2	The Right Blend	82
Figure 4.1	Loco Fedora at Danbury's First Night 2011	98
Figure 4.2	Traveling Men	99
Figure 4.3	SUREFIRE!	102
Figure 4.4	Real Chemistry	105

Acknowledgements

Writing this book has only been possible with the help of many people, within and outside the confines of the Danbury Mad Hatters. The Chapter files archived at the Church of Christ at 90 Clapboard Ridge Road in Danbury, the current rehearsal space, were an important starting point. I would like to thank Bob Connolley, Jack Cramer, Anton Grosz, Jim Hopper, Joe Hudson, Bill Manion, Dick Walter, and Dick Zang for agreeing to be interviewed as part of this project, and to Bob Stewart for his helpful emails. Special thanks go to Bill Manion and Dick Zang for being willing to field so many follow-up phone calls. Thanks to Bob Bartley and Bob Connolley for sending me so much wonderful information to add to the project. Thank you to the Traveling Men for understanding when I was twice late to rehearsal while completing parts of the book. Thanks to Brian Stevens, University Archivist at Western Connecticut State University, who generously helped me find materials on the chorus in the Truman Warner Papers. Thanks to my wife Sujata Gadkar-Wilcox, who was patient when I spent late nights writing this, and my daughters Ishika and Aksita, who waited for their daddy to play with them while he was inserting the photos. This book could not have been produced without the tireless editing assistance of Dick Zang, and without Andy Bayer's invaluable proofreading and advice on many different drafts. Most importantly, thanks go to the men of the Mad Hatter Chorus, past and present, who have afforded me the privilege of being your Vice President of Music and Assistant Director. One could search far and wide and not find a nicer bunch of guys. This book is dedicated to all of you.

1 No Message, Just Pleasure
The Early Years, 1966–1973

On July 12, 1966, the Board of Directors of the nascent Danbury Mad Hatter Barbershop Chorus convened to discuss preparations to become organized and chartered as an official chapter of the Society for the Preservation and Encouragement of Barbershop Quartet Singing in America (SPEBSQSA). The effort to organize a Danbury Barbershop Chapter had started in December 1965, and interest had grown following two organizational meetings in the spring of 1966. Astoundingly, in just six months, the Mad Hatters became a thirty-seven-member chorus, led by organizer and President Edward C. Firmender of Pleasant Rise in Brookfield and Secretary Ray Wixted of South Street in Danbury.

In the late 1940s or early 1950s, an attempt to organize a chapter in Danbury had failed. Yet this time, a relatively large chorus was organized quickly. There is no one simple reason for the change in fortune between the unsuccessful Mad Hatter Chorus of the 1940s or 1950s and the successful Mad Hatter Chorus of the 1960s, but there were multiple contributing factors. First, barbershop music experienced a second resurgence in the mid-1960s. The first revival of barbershop had occurred in 1938, when O. C. Cash brought luminaries, acquaintances, and friends together on the roof garden of the Tulsa club in Tulsa, Oklahoma for an evening of tongue-in-cheek Barbershop merriment that made fun both of the Roosevelt administration's New Deal policies and the byzantine initiation rituals of male fraternal orders. This movement eventually led to the founding of SPEBSQSA.[1] The organization, which had faltered during World War II when so many of its potential members were overseas, experienced yet another renaissance in the 1960s, fueled by the popularity of the musical (and later film) *The Music Man*, anxiety over cultural change and the Cold War, and a longing for a simpler past. In particular, founding members of the Danbury Mad Hatters Chorus remembered *The Music Man* as playing a role in sparking enthusiasm for barbershop.[2]

Transformations of the Danbury area also increased the fledgling Danbury Chapter's prospects for success. In the 1950s, Danbury was still trying to shift its identity from the small hat-making industrial center it had been for nearly a century into a haven for high-technology industries with easy access to New York. Its hopes of an easy transition, however, were dashed in the summer and fall of 1955, when the polluted Still River twice overflowed its banks, destroying both the dying hat factories in the center of the city and many of the new businesses. The economy of the Danbury area would take years to recover.[3] Arguably, the immediate downtown area of Danbury, as represented by Main Street, would never be fully restored to its pre-1955 glory.

By 1966, however, much had changed. The high-tech boom that had been stalled by the 1955 floods had begun to rise again. Danbury was able to take advantage of federal disaster relief money to rebuild and attract new industry. The fifteen-mile stretch of what would become Interstate 84, from the New York State line to Sandy Hook, Connecticut, was opened in 1961, and it was extended to Waterbury in 1963. In 1968, the opening of what would become Interstate 684 made the Danbury area accessible for commuting to New York.[4] Danbury was no longer a center of industrial or agricultural production. Replacing this old Danbury was a new and expanded greater Danbury area. In this era, greater Danbury was becoming a bedroom community for lower Fairfield county and New York. It also became hub for new technology and engineering firms.

Some founding members of the Mad Hatters, such as future director Raymond "Ray" Wixted (1937–2012), hailed from venerable Danbury-area families. Many others, however, were new arrivals to the Danbury area. They were attracted by jobs in aeronautics, engineering, or other technical fields. Some were looking to settle in a location away from the hustle and bustle of larger cities. Many of them were young professionals. Those trends produced favorable demographic conditions for establishing and maintaining a robust membership for the chapter. The exploding population of young families, which fueled a massive expansion in school building and construction in the Danbury area, also brought to Danbury men early in their careers who were seeking the social outlet that barbershop harmony would offer them.

The late 1960s were a time of great cultural fervor, and Danbury was often at the center of it. Fans of the Doors remember a raucous concert held at the auditorium of Danbury High School in October 1967—the same auditorium in which the Mad Hatters of that era most frequently performed. The Doors brought the counterculture to Danbury in force, and bootleg tapes of their seminal Danbury concert are still very much in demand.[5] In addition, in 1971, years of racial tension that had built up amongst students and faculty exploded in race riots at Danbury High.[6] The chorus appears to have been understood as an escape for some from the political tensions of the era. A reporter from the *Danbury News-Times* commented prior to the 1969 Annual Show that the selling point of barbershop was that it offered "no message, just pleasure": pleasure of listening to a solid musical performance without having to endorse a political message, during an era in which musical performance had become increasingly politicized at the height of the folk revival and of songs protesting the Vietnam War.[7]

Despite this larger historical context, most of the extraordinary success of the early Mad Hatter Chorus can be attributed to the careful organization of its founders. The organizers of the Mad Hatters also benefited from SPEBSQSA's assistance. In the late summer of 1966, a delegation from the society headquarters, then in Kenosha, Wisconsin, came to visit with the organizing committee and advised them on repertoire, publicity, and organization—something that the effort to organize an earlier chapter in the 1950s had lacked.[8] The original organizational meeting was held on March 9, 1966 at the Danbury Motor Inn, and featured singing from members of the Bridgeport chapter, which was then called the Ringmaster Chorus.[9] By July 12, 1966, the Mad Hatters had a core organizing board of five people: Ed Firmender, Dick Beckner, Victor Marino, James Kovacs, and Bill Kearney. On that night, the first meeting from which there are minutes, the applications of four more founding members were approved: Robert Conti, John Martino, Joe Talarico, and Joe Speglevin.[10] On, September 10, 1966, less than two months later, SPEBSQSA presented the Mad Hatter Charter to the thirty-seven "charter" members and they gave their very first performance.[11]

The Mad Hatters were able to successfully organize and present their performance at Charter Night due to the ingenuity and resourcefulness of their organizers. Ed Firmender (1930–2015), the founder of the organization, had been a member of the Bridgeport Chorus. He had just recently moved to Brookfield. A jovial man who was also born in Bridgeport, Firmender had moved to the recently constructed houses on Pleasant Rise in Brookfield, just above majestic Candlewood Lake. He ran a popular A & W Root Beer drive-in on Federal Road in Danbury. When the early Mad Hatters, who could hardly afford to spend money on uniforms, were in need of something to wear, Firmender cleverly fashioned the red-and-white striped A & W outfits into the Mad Hatters' first, and perhaps their most memorable, uniforms.[12]

Having met with the team from Kenosha and passed inspection, the Mad Hatters were officially chartered on August 31, 1966.[13] To celebrate the occasion, the Mad Hatters organized their first show, the Charter Night celebration, for September 10, 1966, at the auditorium of the new Danbury High School on Clapboard Ridge Road in Danbury. The road to the Charter night show was not altogether smooth. The Bridgeport

Chapter, which was supposed to be the sponsor of the new chorus, almost pulled out from sponsorship for reasons that are unclear. In July, the Board voted to approve changing the sponsor to the Elm City Chorus

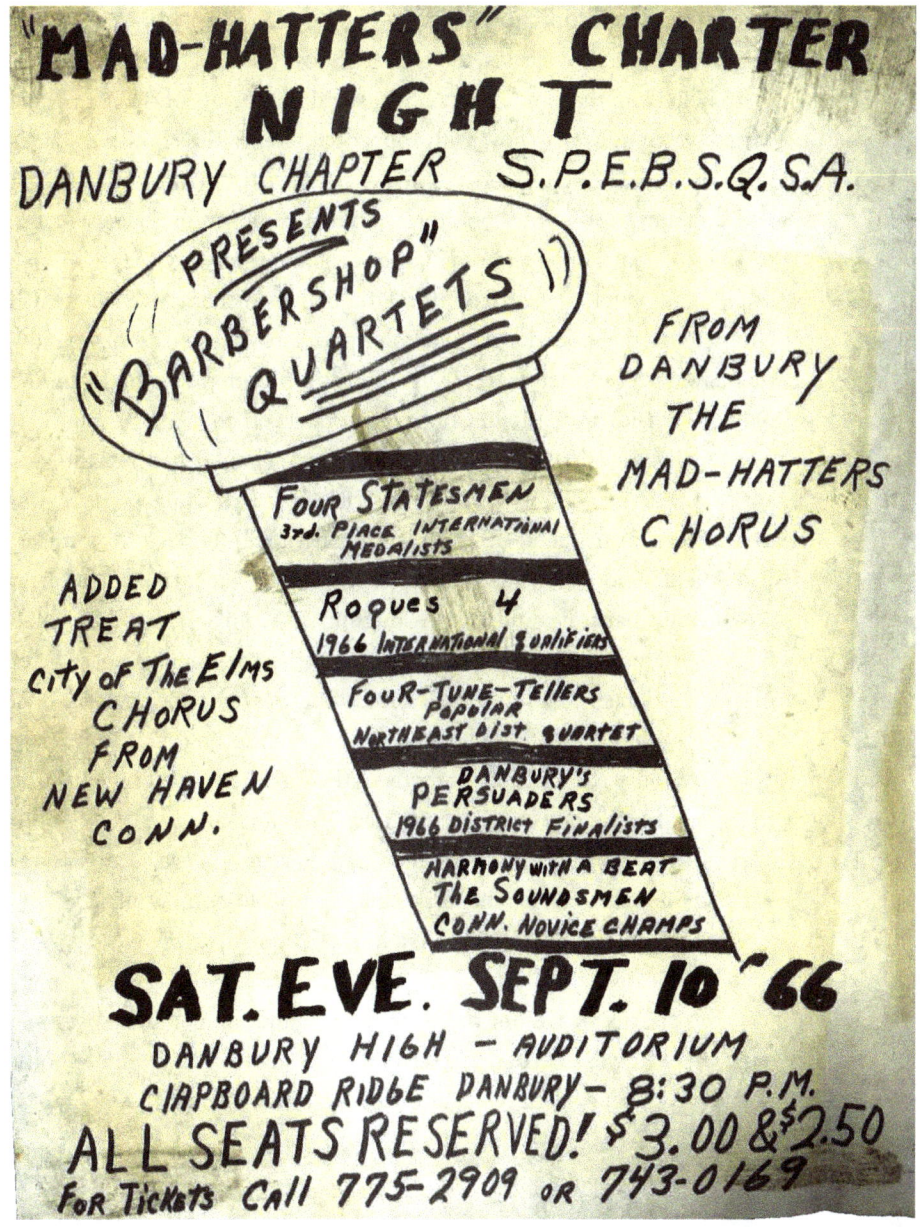

1.1 *Charter Night Flyer*

in New Haven, which came to sing at the Charter Show.[14] A music director needed to be found, but the chorus was not yet in a position to pay whichever person was chosen. By mid-summer, chorus conduct rules were not set; by-laws were not written; and attorneys had not been contacted about incorporation papers.[15]

Despite these obstacles, the Charter Show was a tremendous success. With help from the New Haven Chorus and the society, the Mad Hatters were able to put on a show with top-notch talent. The show was headlined by the Four Statesmen, a Northeastern District (NED) quartet that had come in third at the 1966 international competition, but was fated to be crowned champion in 1967, the very next year. The Rogues Four, a popular regional quartet from the Poughkeepsie chapter that had also competed at the 1966 international, also performed, as well as the Soundsmen, a quartet of men from Bridgeport and Meriden who had won the Novice Division at the 1966 Connecticut Division contest.

Finally, the show featured Danbury's own chapter quartet, the Persuaders, who had qualified for the District finals as a Bridgeport chapter quartet earlier in the year.[16] The Persuaders included Jack Williams of Brookfield, tenor; Joe Millett of Bridgeport, lead; Chuck Fisk of Plainfield, New Jersey, baritone; and Clark Coughlin of Monroe, bass.[17] The Mad Hatters themselves would take the stage under the direction of charter member Michael Noto (b. 1922), a founding member and the founding director of the chorus. The chorus had been "rehearsing" for five months at the Danbury Motor Inn, but many of the members had joined just the month or two before the Charter show. Therefore, they sang only once at the beginning of the show, later joining in as members of the Poughkeepsie and New Haven chapters sang mostly old and familiar barbershop songs, including "Cuddle Up a Little Closer," "Wagon Wheels," and "Side by Side."[18]

The chorus was about more than the founding members' personal enjoyment. It was also dedicated to the assistance of the Danbury community. Al Maino, the President of the NED and Master of Ceremonies

1.2 Receiving the Charter

at the first Charter night show, stressed that the Mad Hatters would be a service organization whose purpose would be to "do good in the community" and "help churches, clubs, and other organizations in fundraising." Consistent with that message, the Charter show also included a "community sing" audience sing-along portion directed by Jack MacGregor of Trumbull, from the Bridgeport chapter, and featured organ music by local musician Emile Buzaid.[19]

Finally, in what would be a highlight of the chorus for decades to come, the informal afterglow was more of a highlight for the community than the show itself. The afterglow was held at the venue that would come to be associated with the chorus for four decades: the Elks Hall on Main Street in Danbury. Nearly the entire crowd proceeded down the hill from the High School to the Elks Hall, filling the cavernous main hall of the building, and demanding encore after encore from the Four Statesmen.[20]

Having put on such a successful Charter Night, Chapter leaders found it difficult to maintain the energy and interest that had initially fueled the organization of the chorus. They therefore searched for new and innovative ways of keeping the chorus growing. At the board meeting in January 1967, the members decided to combine an inter-chapter evening and a membership-building guest night. Quartets and the choruses from Poughkeepsie and Bridgeport were invited to the Elks Club, and members were promised a meeting with plenty of free-flowing alcohol. However, the chapter's Board of Directors specified that Danbury chapter members could only get into the inter-chapter if they came with the price of admission: another man potentially interested in joining the chorus.[21]

The inter-chapter and guest night was preceded with a dinner to install officers. That event, which was held in February 1967 at the Danbury Motor Inn, also involved a long night of dancing. In that year, the Mad Hatters initiated a long-standing practice of holding picnics, later called "backyard singouts," at the homes of members, ensuring excellent food

1.3 *The Persuaders performing in 1966*

and plenty of legal beverages, while inviting neighbors and community members to join.[22] Consequently, by mid-1967, the membership of the chorus had increased to forty-five men.[23] The Danbury group had another motivation to keep the momentum going in 1967: its very own chapter quartet, the Persuaders, had won the 1966 NED Championship and were on their way to the 1967 International Contest, to be held in Los Angeles in July. On June 17, just a few weeks before the contest, the chapter held a "songfest" to send them off, with proceeds going to defray the expenses incurred by the quartet at international.[24] The quartet went on to perform admirably at international, placing thirty-sixth in a crowded field of competitors.

Bill Manion, who would later become (several times) the musical Director of the Mad Hatters, remembers his first chapter meeting in the fall of 1967. He and Ed Ryder (a future Mad Hatter president) had heard through the grapevine about the new barbershop group in town and decided to travel down to the Danbury Motor Inn to check them out. As Manion recalls, "it so happened that the Persuaders were there that night in the motel on Main Street where they rehearsed. Their sound blew me away, and I was hooked."[25]

Despite these highlights, the first full year of operations did present challenges for the Mad Hatters. In the summer of 1967, the Danbury Motor Inn began to institute a charge for meetings that was more than the chapter could pay, forcing the chapter to move meetings down the street to the Elks Lodge. This move reflected the still-tight finances of the new group. Morale was also harder to maintain as more potential members were rejected for not having singing skills that "measured up to [the] organization's standards."[26] In the very terse minutes of the board meeting of June 4, 1967, the financial problems were coming to a head in preparation for the songfest later in the month and the annual show, to be held in September of that year. The chapter was struggling to pay for performance rights for songs, and to produce programs. At the same time, interest among the rank and file barbershoppers was beginning to wane.

In response to these potential problems, the Board voted to radically change the way that rehearsals would be conducted. Starting in the summer of 1967, formal rehearsals would begin sharply at eight o'clock. Rehearsals would last only ninety minutes. Following each rehearsal would be a program of singing from quartets. Informally, the festivities would continue in the Elks Lodge's basement Rathskeller, which one member described as the epitome of an old-style "typical smoke-filled bar."[27] In the Rathskeller, singing and drinking continued late into the night. After midnight, singers would continue to congregate outside the Elks Lodge, woodshedding in the cold. Some would even head down Interstate 84 to New York State, where bars could be found open until 2am, to continue their singing late into the night, almost until the morning.[28]

Over time, the revelry and merriment, and the endless woodshedding and quartetting (not to mention the drinking), that would accompany the end of every rehearsal, characterize every "backyard singout," and would punctuate every afterglow, gave Danbury a reputation as the most entertaining and hospitable chapter in the division. Danbury developed a reputation for hosting memorable inter-chapter evenings and outstanding afterglows at division and district competitions, complete with top-notch food and top-shelf drinks.[29] This routine became so popular that in the early 1970s, the chorus had to eliminate having intermissions at their regular rehearsals because too many members would retire to the Rathskeller at halftime and not come back up for the second half of the rehearsal.[30]

This dynamic of the chorus remained the most important driving force in maintaining interest and membership from the late 1960s to the pinnacle of the Mad Hatters in the mid-to-late 1970s, when membership reached as high as ninety-nine members. The appeal of this informal woodshedding and quart singing reflected both the demographics of the chapter and the society at large that made such male social bonding possible and desirable. Members of the chorus were relatively young, white middle-class professionals with some expendable income. They were mostly married men with careers and families. An official roster from February 1971 revealed the mean year of birth of a Mad Hatter Chorus member to be 1929, placing the average member between forty-one and forty-two years of age at the time.[31]

Moreover, the late 1960s were still an era in which most of these young male professionals were the single income earners for their families. By the late 1970s, members of male-dominated organizations such as veterans' associations and fraternal orders would decline drastically.[32] As a result, the membership rolls in SPEBSQSA, and in the Danbury Chapter, would suffer a similar fate. Between 1954 and 1976, Barbershop society membership grew at an annual rate of 0.9 percent; between 1976 and 1988, it would decline at a rate of 0.86 percent annually.[33] The impressive increase in interest in barbershop activities from the mid-1950s to the mid-1970s, followed by its precipitous decline, tracks with another major change in American society: the feminist movement and the concomitant introduction of a critical mass of women into the labor force.

From the 1970s until the 2000s, the proportion of employed adult men actually declined from 81 percent to 75 percent, while the number of women participating in the labor force increased from 44 percent to 60 percent.[34] Sociologist Scott Coltrane has suggested that the growth of all-male activities in this time period was a reaction against such changes.[35] Just as fraternal organizations rose to prominence at the turn of the twentieth century in the context of the emergence of the suffrage movement, so too the expansion of Barbershop Chapters in the 1960s and 1970s may have reflected a nostalgia for male gathering and bonding spaces just as some of the conditions for the possibility for such late-night caterwauling—the male breadwinner family structure—were being undermined.

One final aspect of the Mad Hatters' emphasis on informal quartetting and of quartet programs at the expense of formal choral rehearsal time during the late 1960s and early 1970s bears mentioning. This was a chapter driven by its membership, and driven by quartet singing. The

Mad Hatters were interested in performing, and did regularly perform. Yet chorus singing was not the primary emphasis of the chapter at this time. Therefore, the Musical Director did not drive the chorus. The chapter in these years was controlled by a powerful Board of Directors, who selected the Director, usually from within the membership. The Director answered to the Board, nearly all of whose members were founders of the Chapter. It did not work the other way around.[36]

As a consequence, the early chapter did not have long-standing directors. For reasons that are not entirely clear, in the spring of 1967 Michael Noto went from being the director of the chorus to the Assistant Director. Ray Wixted, a young history teacher at New Fairfield High School who had directed local church choirs, assumed the mantle of Music Director.[37] Wixted's first tenure, however, was short-lived. In November 1968, he declared himself unavailable for further directing and was replaced by Bill Manion (b. 1930) and Don Sutherland (1929–2016), who acted as Co-Directors.[38] This would be the first of several tenures at the helm for Manion, and he would remain there until Anton Grosz took over in January 1973. In the summer of 1969, the arrangement changed slightly, with Manion as Director and Sutherland as Assistant Director.[39] In December 1971, Al Thompson joined Sutherland as a second Assistant Director.[40]

Under Wixted's direction, the Mad Hatters held their second annual show, "Night of Harmony," at Danbury High School on September 19, 1967. The immensely popular Four Statesmen, now International Champions, returned. Rocket Tones, an international finalist quartet from New Jersey, accompanied them, as did the Persuaders and the Soundsmen, a comedy quartet from the Bridgeport Chapter. Making their debut on the 1967 show were the Nutmeggers, a popular late 1960s chapter quartet. The program continued to feature a "community sing" directed by Jack MacGregor. The Elks Hall featured an afterglow, at which the quartets "let their hair down," with a $2.00 buffet, beginning at the late hour of 11:30pm.[41]

1.4 *The Nutmeggers*

From 1968 through 1971, under the direction of Bill Manion, the chorus tried to maintain and expand on its developing reputation for fun and camaraderie while simultaneously improving singing performance and continuing to build community. Manion was a prominent nuclear engineer and was the President of Nuclear Energy Services, a private engineering firm in Danbury, whom the press occasionally called upon to explain matters related to nuclear power.[42] Manion was a reluctant director. He had just joined the chapter in 1967 and was not one of the charter members. He was a good piano player and could therefore read music, but had no other formal musical training. Upon becoming Director, he set about learning how to direct by attending the rehearsals of the Poughkeepsie New Yorkers Chorus. At that time, the Poughkeepsie chorus was one of the best in the society. Under the direction of Bill James, Poughkeepsie, which had only been chartered in 1961, won the NED Chorus Contest in 1964, 1965, 1968, and 1969. In that year, they placed sixth at international.[43] Bill James subjected Manion to a trial by fire. Upon coming to Poughkeepsie to observe the chorus, he was almost immediately put in front of this excellent chorus to direct songs.[44] With this more informal training, Manion quickly learned how to direct.

In 1968, the Mad Hatters held a parade to fund a science laboratory for St. Peter's school in Danbury. It featured the Nutmeggers; the Unlikely Hoods, a very buttoned-up, turtleneck-wearing quartet from Poughkeepsie; and the Four-Tune-Tellers of New Haven, as well as the chorus. The Danbury chorus delighted the audience with traditional barbershop songs such as "I'll Take You Home Kathleen," and "Oh We Don't Have a Barrel of Money" as well as a rousing rendition of "California Here I Come." The stars, however, were the Nutmeggers, who "really won the full admiration of the audience," many of whom had not had the opportunity to see them before. In the mind of Danbury News-Times reporter Lynne Royce, the event, officially called the "Saint Peter's Guild Chordbuster's Parade of Barbershop Harmony," offered a welcome respite from the troubling winds of social change whipping the country in the early summer of 1968: "Problems like whom to vote for in the presidential election and what is going on at the peace talks in Paris were momentarily forgotten."[45] That spirit was also on hand at the September 1968 annual show, "Barbershopping in the Park," featuring the Rocket-Tones, the Nutmeggers, and the Harmo-Nuts, a comedy quartet from the Framingham, Massachusetts, Chapter.

The shift from concentrating on local shows to focusing on performance occurred in 1969. At their July 1969 meeting, the Board discussed the possibility of continuing to sell more package shows to corporations and local entities, which had been done in the previous years, or to focus on the Annual Show. Though the discussion appears to have been inconclusive, and some attempts were made to solicit the purchase of more package shows from corporate sponsors, in reality such activities from that time seemed to have decreased.[46] At the very next meeting of the Board, the chapter expressed a commitment to attend the Division chorus competition in March 1970, and began to look into the possibility of holding a competition in Danbury.[47]

In the midst of the increased focus on singing, the Mad Hatters moved up their annual show to May in 1969, and dedicated a portion of the proceeds to benefit a non-profit association with the dated and not politically correct name "The Danbury Association to Advance the Handicapped and Retarded." The show was held as usual at the auditorium at Danbury High School. It featured the New Yorkers chorus from Poughkeepsie, the reigning Northeastern District Champions, co-directed by Bill James and Steve Plumb. The show featured the Nutmeggers and a Bridgeport/Danbury quartet called the Noblemen, with Tom Dardis on tenor, Hank Seymore on lead, Bud Wallick on baritone, and Pete Zerrelly on bass. In addition, the show highlighted two very good quartets from Poughkeepsie. The first, the Homesteaders, included the future director of the Mad Hatters, Anton Grosz, on bass, as well as Steve Plumb on baritone, Bruce Slack on tenor, and Don Krieger on lead. The second, the Rouges Four, was a popular Northeastern District quartet with Aubrey Light on tenor, Bill James on lead, Art Burns on baritone, and Fritz Jones on bass.[48] With Ray Wixted as Master of Ceremonies, the Mad Hatters took the first half performing "Yona from Arizona," "The Banjo's Back in Town" and "I'll Take You Home Again Kathleen." The Poughkeepsie chorus led the Community Sing in the second half. At the performance, the work at improving the Mad Hatters was evident in Lynne Royce's reporting that the chorus now sounded polished and professional. It was a nostalgic night, in Royce's words, during which "problems of taxes, inflation, student rebellion, the war in Vietnam, and other national crises were wiped away by the brotherhood and harmony of the barbershoppers."[49]

Another early show highlight was the 1971 annual show, "Gay 90's Revue," featuring the comedy quartets The Note-Wits from Livingston,

New Jersey, and the Two Plus Two Four from Richmond, Virginia, as well as a well-received women's quartet from the Stamford, Connecticut, Sweet Adelines chapter. The show also featured three chapter quartets, including the locally popular Yankee Peddlers. The Peddlers sang in various configurations through the mid-1970s, but this version featured Jack Williams on tenor, Ray Schetler on lead, Jim Hopper on baritone, and Bill Manion on bass. Jim Hopper, who was with the chorus from 1969 to 1973 and was secretary in 1970–1971, briefly re-joined the chorus in 1994 and then re-joined for good in 2002, and continues to be an integral member. Hopper, Manion, and Williams would join forces in other quartets over the years as well.[50]

The Division III Chorus Contest in Shelton, CT on March 14, 1970, was the first competition in which the Mad Hatters appear to have competed as a chorus. The Mad Hatters sang "On the Sunny Side of the Street" and "That Old Gang of Mine." They placed eighth out of eleven choruses in the contest, and did not qualify for districts, at a time during which the Connecticut Division was quite competitive. The Mad Hatters scored very well in the Harmony Accuracy category, coming in third behind the district's top two choruses, New London and Meriden. But the chorus was given low marks for its delivery and presentation, as well as its musical precision. Members were not smiling; dynamic contrast was not sufficient; and singing was a bit too choppy. A twenty-five-point penalty was assessed because of the shoddy quality of the uniforms. Members had pant legs of very different lengths. In the 1971 division competition, the chorus improved slightly, placing seventh.

Under the leadership of President Lawrence Taylor and Director Bill Manion, in the summer of 1971 the chapter made a commitment to improve singing by adopting a two-chorus system. There was now a sing-in chorus, in which every member would participate, and a sing-out chorus, for which a committee, appointed by the Board of Directors, imposed rigorous qualifications. Additionally, a program to aid members in meeting the qualifications was instituted. As it was a matter of great

1.5 (opposite) Program Cover of the 1971 Annual Show

Danbury Chapter, SPEBSQSA

presents a

Gay 90's Revue

Saturday, May 1, 1971

8 P. M.

Danbury High School Auditorium

1.6 Bill Manion directing the Mad Hatter Chorus in 1971

importance, the two-chorus system was put to a vote of the entire chorus, and was approved.[51]

The new qualifications were typed and distributed to the chapter. They specified that "these requirements are not aimed at excluding any member from participating in chorus performances." The qualifications were only supposed to ensure that each member was making the requisite effort, and to "prevent the individual who is not willing to work from destroying our performances." Even small groups, such as the thirteen-man chorus from Pittsfield, Massachusetts, could "make a fine sound." The author asserted that the Mad Hatters should "stop cheating [them]selves."[52]

To qualify to "sing out" at events or contests, each member would have to demonstrate to "a minimum of three members of the qualification committee" that he could sing the correct words and music to each sing-out chorus song either as a solo, in duet with a lead, or in a "quartet of his choosing." Each member was given four weeks after a song was introduced to the chorus to learn his part. This requirement was controversial enough that in the archived copy, a member had scribbled a question mark and asked incredulously in the margin in pencil: "How does he ever qualify after four weeks?" In addition, members were required to maintain a 75% attendance rate, and know that their status as sing-in or sing-out chorus members would be posted.[53]

Having strengthened and clarified their expectations of members, the Mad Hatters were in a position to improve at the 1972 Division Contest, which they hosted. However, the qualifications proved difficult to implement. The process moved slowly in the fall of 1971, but picked up speed

1.7 *The Mad Hatters performing on their 1971 Annual Show*

in 1972 after section leaders were directed to spend more time on the activity.[54] Reflecting the new focus on competition, the chapter ordered new navy blue double-breasted jackets and white trousers to improve the uniform.[55] In addition, at rehearsal night each Tuesday in February 1972, Director Bill Manion brought a different contest judge to the chorus for coaching. Ray Wixted also brought Ona May, a noted choreographer of barbershop choruses, to the meetings to improve moves.[56] These efforts bore fruit in 1972. Sporting new blazers, the chorus placed fifth in the divisional contest that year, and their efforts at advancement, recruitment, and retention in the chapter—what the Society at the time was promoting as their Protention Program—was featured in the society magazine, the *Harmonizer*.[57]

1972 also saw the rise of a new chapter quartet, one that would be remembered as perhaps the finest of the Mad Hatter's history: the Lavender Hill Mob, featuring Ray Wixted on tenor, John Ahearn on lead, Dick Hess on baritone, and Tony Grosz—then not yet affiliated with the Danbury chapter, still only with Poughkeepsie—on bass.[58] That year, a banner year for the Northeastern district, four of its quartets qualified for the International Contest: Boston Common, the 1971 district champions and 1980 International Champions, Grandma's Boys, the 1979 International Champions, the 1966 District Champions the Adventurers, and the 1972 District Champions, the Penthouse Four. The Lavender Hill Mob, which had just come into existence, placed ninth and was an alternate to international. In the meantime, the Danbury chorus, making their first appearance at Districts, became second alternates to international.[59]

Under the direction of Tony Grosz and Ray Wixted, the Mad Hatters would enjoy the pinnacle of their success in the late 1970s and early 1980s, winning the division and twice placing fifth in the Northeastern District that was at the time one of the most competitive districts in the society. Yet surely a great deal of the credit for the competitive success of the chapter should be properly given to Bill Manion, under whose leadership a program of competitive success became possible.

1.8 (opposite) *The Lavender Hill Mob*

While working to strengthen their musical skills, the Mad Hatters found ways to retain their main strength: their reputation as the most fun chapter in the district. They were the chapter of madcap antics. Bill Manion himself, despite his work on making the Danbury chapter a place of more "serious" fun, certainly is remembered for having a humorous side. In addition to a hilarious tendency, undoubtedly attributable to his scientific background, to take things far too literally, Bill Manion is the source of an oft-repeated piece of Danbury lore: if a Mad Hatter forgets the words of a song during a performance, he is simply to softly repeat "banana, banana, banana" while singing the right notes, and few audience members will ever notice.[60]

In addition to their jovial director, the chorus found two other ways to highlight their fun factor. The first was to increase their backyard

singouts. During the summer of 1972, backyard singouts were held nearly twice a month. This appears also to be the first time that they were hosted by Joe Talarico (1908–1989).[61] While perhaps not the best singer in the group, Talarico was the emotional center of the Mad Hatters in the 1970s and 1980s. He was famous for hosting backyard events with food so fantastic that his entire block would fill with guests. He would then place himself in the center of the entertainment. As an expressive man whom everyone knew, he would become a one-man public relations dynamo for the chorus.[62]

The other innovation that dates to 1972 is the Mad Hatter Ladies' Auxiliary, which was suggested by founding member Thomas Dardis. The purpose of the Auxiliary was to "furnish aid during chapter functions and esprit-de-corps during competitions—sort of a ladies' cheering section." At the August 1972 meeting where this was proposed, however, it caused a heated debate amongst members about the desirability of the participation of women in chapter functions and was actually voted down with eight board members voting "no," one voting "yes," and one abstention.[63] The Ladies' Auxiliary was raised and not carried again at the October 1972 board meeting. Eventually, however, it became an informal reality and was remembered as the reason for the success of chapter-run afterglows and for creating a positive atmosphere in which to sing.[64]

At the first Board meeting in 1973, Tony Grosz, who had been singing with three members of the Danbury chapter with the Lavender Hill Mob, was formally voted in as the new chapter music director, ushering in a new era of expansion of the chorus. This formalized a transition that had already occurred informally: Grosz had in fact been directing the chorus since the fall of 1972.[65] He was to be paid $5.00 per rehearsal for his directing. This appears to be the first time a director was paid.[66] The chapter also paid his society membership dues, beginning a tradition that would last to the present day.[67] Grosz would set the chorus up for the pinnacle of success that would be reached under Ray Wixted.

1.9 Sweater patch of the Mad Hatter Chorus, designed by illustrator Frank Golden

Notes

1 Gage Averill, *Four Parts, No Waiting: A Social History of American Barbershop Harmony* (New York: Oxford University Press, 2003), 99–100.

2 *Ibid.*, 151–152; For the Music Man's influence on the founders of the Mad Hatter Chorus specifically, Frank Merkling, "Madhatters: 83 in Four-Part Harmony," *The News-Times* (June 8, 1982):9.

3 William E. Devlin and Herbert F. Janick, *Danbury's Third Century: From Urban Status to Tri-Centennial* (Danbury, CT: Western Connecticut State University, 2013), 229–232.

4 *Ibid.*, 260–261.

5 Libor Jany, "45 Years Ago, Doors Left Mark on Danbury," *Connecticut Post* (November 10, 2012), A1; Gary Freeman, *The Bootleg Guide: Classic Bootlegs of the 1960s and 1970s* (Lanham, MD: Scarecrow Press, 2003), 183.

6 Nick Fraticelli, "Danbury High School's 1971 Crimson Wave of Violence: Its Causes and Effects," *Clio: WCSU History Journal* (2006):93.

7 Lynne Royce, "No Message, Just Pleasure from Barbershop Concert," *Danbury News-Times* (May 12, 1969), 19.

8 Merkling, "Madhatters: 83 in Four-Part Harmony," 9. According to Ray Wixted's recollections in Markling's news article, the effort to organize a chapter in the 1950s was hindered by a sentiment that barbershop music was actually "too modern" for the classical sensibilities prevailing at the time.

9 "Barbershoppers Will Organize," *Danbury News-Times* (March 3, 1966), 1.

10 Minutes of Board of Directors, Danbury Chorus, July 12, 1966.

11 Charter Show Flyer and Insert, Danbury Mad Hatter Scrapbook 1966–1980.

12 Bill Manion, personal interview, March 17, 2016.

13 "Our New Chapters," *The Harmonizer* XXVI:6 (Dec.1966):26.

14 Ultimately, it appears that the Bridgeport chapter remained the sponsor, though the New Haven Chapter, not the Bridgeport Chapter, sang on the chapter show. Hank Yazdzik of Shelton, Bridgeport Chapter President, was present at the Chapter Show to present the chapter formally. One might speculate that Bridgeport may have feared losing several members, such as the

members of the Persuaders Quartet, to the new Danbury chapter, whereas the Elm City Chorus was too far away from Danbury to have similar concerns.

15 Minutes of Board of Directors, Danbury Chorus, July 12, 1966.

16 Charter Show Flyer and Insert," Mad Hatter Scrapbook; Lynne Benedict, "Mad-Hatter Barbershoppers Get Charter, Give Harmony at D.H.S.," *Danbury News-Times* (September 12, 1966).

17 "Barber Shop Harmony Will Ring from High School Saturday Night," *Danbury News-Times* (September 7, 1966).

18 Benedict, "Mad-Hatter Barbershoppers Get Charter"

19 *Ibid.*

20 *Ibid.*

21 Minutes of Board of Directors, Danbury Chorus, January 9, 1967.

22 Minutes of Board of Directors, Danbury Chorus, May 1, 1967.

23 Mary Shawah, "Off the Cuff Jottings," *The Bridgeport Post* (July 9, 1967), 16.

24 *Ibid.*

25 Bill Manion, "Letter to the Editor," *Hatter Chatter* 21:8 (October 2014):2; Bill Manion, March 17, 2016.

26 Minutes of Board of Directors, Danbury Chorus, May 1, 1967.

27 Jim Hopper, personal interview, March 10, 2016.

28 Dick Zang, personal interview, February 16, 2016; Bill Manion, personal interview, March 17, 2016.

29 Dick Zang, personal interview, February 16, 2016; Dick Walter, personal interview, February 21, 2016.

30 Bob Connolley, personal interview, April 20, 2016.

31 Membership Roster, SPEBSQSA, February 28, 1971, Form DP-201, 1966–1973 documents binder, Mad Hatter Chorus Archive.

32 Claude S. Fischer, *Still Connected: Family and Friends in America since 1970* (New York: Russell Sage Foundation, 2011), 43.

33 Robert A. Stebbins, *The Barbershop Singer: Inside the Social World of a Musical Hobby* (Toronto: University of Toronto Press, 1996), 88.

34 Fischer, Still Connected, 42.

35 Scott Coltrane, *Family Man: Fatherhood, Housework, and Gender Equality* (New York: Oxford University Press, 1997), 195.

36 Dick Zang, personal interview, February 16, 2016.

37 "Danbury Mad Hatters Present an Evening of Harmony," (Annual Show Program Book, September 16, 1967), 2; Linda Martelli, "Music Keys Wixted," *The News-Times* (November 27, 1977), 1.

38 Minutes of Board of Directors, Danbury Chorus, Nov 27, 1968.

39 Minutes of Board of Directors, Danbury Chorus, July 28, 1969.

40 Minutes of Board of Directors, Danbury Chorus, Dec 2, 1971.

41 "Barbershop Quartet's 'Night of Harmony' September 16th," *Journal-Advertiser* (September 5, 1967), 3; "An Evening of Harmony," (Program Book), 4–6.

42 "N.U.: Chernobyl Won't Be Repeated Here," *The Hour* (April 30, 1986):2.

43 "History," *Newyorkers Chorus*. Retrieved May 2, 2016. http://www.newyorkerschorus.org/id8.html.

44 Bill Manion, personal interview, May 2, 2016.

45 Lynne Royce, "Audience Sings along with Barbershoppers," *Danbury News-Times* (1969).

46 Minutes of Board of Directors, Danbury Chorus, July 28, 1969 and August 25, 1969.

47 Minutes of Board of Directors, Danbury Chorus, Sept 29, 1969.

48 "Barbershopping in the Park," (Annual Show Program Book, May 10, 1969), 1–5.

49 Lynne Royce, "No Message, Just Pleasure," 1.

50 "Gay 90's Revue," (Annual Show Program Book, May 1, 1971), 4; "Barbershop Harmony Hits High Note in 'Gay 90s Revue,'" Danbury News-Times (May 3, 1971); Jim Hopper, personal interview, March 10, 2016.

51 Minutes of Board of Directors, Danbury Chorus, May 13, 1971.

52 The Madhatters Sing-Out Chorus," 1966–1973 documents binder, Danbury Mad Hatter Chorus Archive, 1.

53 *Ibid.*

54 Minutes of Board of Directors, Danbury Chorus, Dec 2, 1971.

55 *Ibid.* Also Minutes of Board of Directors, Danbury Chorus, January 6, 1972.

56 *Ibid.*

57 Al Thomson, "Protention Stimulant for Danbury, Conn.," *The Harmonizer* 32:6 (November 1972):20.

58 At the time, Anton Grosz spelled his last name "Gross." In the 1990s, he legally changed the spelling of his last name at the request of his son; I have retained the changed spelling in this book.

59 "Official Scoring Summary, Int'l Preliminary Quartet Contest and Alternate Chorus Contest," NED, Framingham, MA, May 6, 1972. 1966–1973 documents binder, Danbury Chorus Archive.

60 Bob Connelley, personal interview, April 20, 2016.

61 Sam Patti, "Summer Activities Memo," (July 2, 1972), 1966–1973 documents binder, Danbury Chorus Archive.

62 Dick Zang, personal interview, February 16, 2016.

63 Minutes of Board of Directors, Danbury Chorus, Dec 2, 1971.

64 Dick Walter, personal interview, February 21, 2016.

65 Mario Merolle, personal communication, August 5, 2016.

66 Minutes of Board of Directors, Danbury Chorus, Dec 2, 1971.

67 Minutes of Board of Directors, Danbury Chorus, February 1, 1973.

2 "More Schmaltz"
The Golden Years of Tony Grosz and Ray Wixted, 1973–1987

News-*Times* art critic Frank Merkling visited a Mad Hatter Chorus rehearsal in early June 1982 in preparation for that year's Annual Show, "To Broadway with Roses." The show would feature the "Rosie set" for which the Mad Hatters would become well known in the early 1980s. That evening, he encountered a chorus with eighty-three members.[1] Though the chorus was not growing, their membership was up from the high thirties and low forties ten years before, which was impressive because it ran counter to the overall trend in the society, in which membership had been declining rather drastically since 1976.[2]

In part, the chorus benefited from favorable demographic trends in the area. Western Connecticut was still growing at a rapid rate. The population of Danbury had increased by almost 29 percent between 1960 and 1970, but it had also grown by 19 percent between 1970 and 1980. Whereas in 1950, around the time when a barbershop group had first been contemplated, Danbury had just over 30,000 residents, by the 1980s it had more than 60,000.[3] In addition to benefiting from the increasing suburbanization of the workforce, Danbury continued to benefit from the introduction of new manufacturing and technology companies in the area. In 1976, Union Carbide, a large chemical manufacturing company that had been based in New York City since its inception in 1917, announced that it was moving to Danbury. It began construction of a massive and architecturally unique corporate complex on Danbury's west side, very close to the New York border, in 1980. Construction was completed in 1982, bringing to Danbury yet another influx of relatively young middle-class men who might have some leisure time on their hands.[4] For this reason, even though the founding members of the chorus were beginning to age, 1982 Chapter President Jack Cramer of Danbury could still boast, "the vast majority of our guys are in their 30s and 40s."[5]

Yet this success cannot be attributed to larger demographic trends alone. The core of the chorus's growth was sparked by the tremendous fun, mischief, and camaraderie for which the Mad Hatters were known from the start, and the emphasis on informal singing in the Rathskeller, the Elks Club's bar, following rehearsals. Another driver of growth was the emerging excellence of the quality of the chorus and the quartets it featured. Frank Merkling's visit to the chorus came in the wake of the Mad Hatters' winning the Division Championship, which amounted, at the time, to their being declared the best chorus in the state. This was the second time that the Mad Hatters won the championship; they had won it previously in 1980. In both 1977 and 1981, the chorus had placed fifth at the Division chorus contest, which in both years was held in Lake Placid, New York. In those years, a fifth place finish in the Northeastern District was no small accomplishment in what was then a very competitive district with 80 chapters.

Though the chorus deserves the credit for this substantial improvement in quality, the impetus came from a string of excellent chorus music directors. Bill Manion had set the stage for this improvement by spearheading rules for preparation to sing in performances and contests. Tony Grosz brought energy and techniques from the top-notch Poughkeepsie chorus, and Ray Wixted brought that energy alive. Wixted, whom Merkling described as "genial and stocky, with wavy silver hair and the air of a leprechaun when he directs," brought energy to the chorus and encouraged them, as he said in the rehearsal in June 1982, to sing with "more schmaltz!"[6]

THE GOLDEN YEARS OF TONY GROSZ AND RAY WIXTED, 1973–1987   31

This story of the meteoric rise in chorus quality and membership in the 1970s and early 1980s has its genesis in late 1972. By that time, Bill Manion, an indefatigable director who had limited barbershop training, decided that he had taken the chorus as far as he could. He began to seek

2.1 Fifth place ribbons from the District Contest, 1977 and 1981

out a new director. At the time, the Poughkeepsie chorus was the place to look for talent. It had two excellent assistants, Steve Plumb and Tony Grosz, both of whom had worked under the highly respected directors Bill James and Bob Royce. With the Poughkeepsie chapter's blessing, Manion contacted both Plumb and Grosz about directing Danbury. Grosz was quite interested. Though Poughkeepsie was more than forty miles away, Grosz was already driving to Danbury on regular occasion to rehearse with the Lavender Hill Mob, the other three members of which were Danbury chapter members. And he was very eager to have the opportunity to direct a chorus on his own.[7]

Tony Grosz was born in the Hell's Kitchen section of Manhattan around the 1930s. As a child, he moved to the Bronx, and then on to Bergen County, New Jersey. Between 1957 and 1965, he earned a BA and MA in Economics from Rutgers University. Grosz and his family moved to the Poughkeepsie area in the late 1960s. By 1972, he had become an Economics Professor at Dutchess Community College, a job that he kept until 1980.[8] Grosz was an accomplished musician and is remembered not only as a dynamic director but one of the best singers to have ever sung with the Danbury chapter. He possessed a booming bass voice and a New York City energy and attitude. Moreover, he brought with him his training under top-notch directors while at Poughkeepsie, which was also a model that had made that chapter a perennial district champion in that era. He brought to Danbury the technique of distributing the chorus into quartets and emphasize that every man in the chorus would have the experience of being in a quartet. He also insisted on a challenging, different, and beautiful repertoire on the theory that such music could attract better singers into the chorus.[9]

Tony Grosz's exciting and dynamic directing had an immediate impact. Dick Zang recalls looking for a new chapter after moving to Sandy Hook, Connecticut, in 1973. He was considering several when he was told by barbershoppers from his former chapter in Manhattan that Grosz was an up-and-coming talent who would take the Danbury chapter far. He attended a Danbury meeting and found that his friends were correct in thinking that Danbury was "going places," and Dick Zang remains an integral member of the chorus to this day.[10]

The chorus was already taking positive steps to increase membership. As part of the chorus's Auditions for Admission program, a slick audio-visual presentation and slide show demonstrating the excitement

2.2 *The Mad Hatter Chorus at the District Competition in Lake Placid, NY, October 1973*

of chorus's events was created. In the spring and summer of 1973, the chorus hosted a clambake and a picnic, both of which were successful. The board had also created a "hoopla committee," which is what the de facto ladies' auxiliary was calling itself, which produced and distributed pom-poms, colorful arm patches, and banners. There was even talk of sponsoring a skydiver as a stunt to promote the chorus at the District Contest.[11]

Also in 1973, the chorus instituted a film night. Its members would invite guests to the Elks Hall to watch previous international barbershop competitions as a means of exciting members about the possibilities for Danbury. The film nights included a promotional slide show about the chorus and a raffle for fundraising purposes.[12] The Chapter introduced a series of "Show Glows" that reproduced the atmosphere of an afterglow —including the open bar and buffet—but also included a band and dancing as well as entertainment from the chorus.[13] These efforts yielded impressive results. In June 1973, the chorus had fifty-one paid members.[14] Throughout the rest of 1973, the chorus reported tremendous interest in its Audition for Admission meetings, which introduced guests to the chorus with streamlined admission procedures. Between November 13 and December 4, 1973, four such meetings were held. Twenty-three guests and four past members interested in being reinstated attended the first interest meeting. The second featured seventeen total guests, seven of who were repeats; fifteen and twelve guests showed up for the additional two.[15]

Chorus membership burgeoned. By the September meeting membership was at fifty-eight; by November, it was sixty-five; by December, it was seventy. By the beginning of 1974, the chorus had seventy-five members. Membership had increased by more than twenty percent in six months. The new membership came in various forms: a resurgence of interest by former members, transfers from other local chapters, and entirely new men. Moreover, the new members included some very good singers. In addition to Dick Zang, new members included Len Carlson, John Ahearn, lead of the Lavender Hill Mob, and future chapter president Jack Cramer.

1973 also featured one notable and memorable performance. Early in the year, Ed Firmender's young son Craig was seriously injured when he accidentally came into contact with high voltage electricity lines, requiring his hospitalization and a long recovery period, which inevitably led to considerable medical bills. The Mad Hatters came to the aid of their founder. On June 9, 1973, the Chapter held a benefit for the Firmenders, along with the Poughkeepsie and Derby chapters, and local quartets, including the Penthouse Four, a Poughkeepsie quartet and the 1972 NED champs.

Events like these kept the Mad Hatters together as a tight-knit group even as they expanded. Yet the real driver remained the quality of the group. Not only did the chorus qualify for districts in Lake Placid in 1973, but they also made the top ten, a particularly impressive feat considering that at the time there were sixty-five competing choruses. At Lake Placid that year, the Lavender Hill Mob came in fourth in the quartet competition.[16] The Mad Hatters were well on their way to becoming something special.

At their January 1974 meeting, the board member realized that the incredibly rapid growth made it difficult to decide who would sing at contest. They decided to not guarantee eligibility for the district contest in March for additional members above the level of seventy-five, not only as a "quality control" measure, but also because they lacked a sufficient number of uniforms.

To keep the momentum going, the chorus, largely on the initiative of the Music Committee and the director Tony Grosz, encouraged good-natured competition and audacious stunts to keep the chorus members on their toes. In February 1974, the Board approved a suggestion from Grosz that "the chorus make a bet with Poughkeepsie on the outcome of the Boston District Contest" in the fall. If Danbury placed within four ranks of Poughkeepsie, then Poughkeepsie would have to sing on Danbury's show for free; if Danbury did not, then they would have to sing on Poughkeepsie's show for free.[17] Danbury did not quite meet this goal at the October districts, placing eleventh while Poughkeepsie placed sixth.[18] However, in successive districts, Danbury would move closer and closer to Poughkeepsie, finally surpassing them in 1977.

Grosz built excitement by promoting feats of stamina. On one day —December 15, 1974—the chorus performed a total of five shows, which was accomplished only by subdividing into two: the "East Chorus," which performed two package shows at retirement homes in Connecticut, and the "West Chorus," which performed at two rest homes in New York, before the chorus as a whole came together for a rehearsal and then to Immaculate High School in Danbury for a Christmas pageant.[19] While this activity sounds exhausting, it was typical of the atmosphere of the challenge, the desire to do what seemed impossible, that fueled the excitement of the chapter in those years.

In the fall of 1974, the chorus also initiated the Danbury Connecticut Quartet Challenge Cup to promote more quartet singing in the region. The Danbury Cup was a challenge to other chapters to come to Danbury with a series of quartets that would participate in a head-to-head competition with the Danbury quartets. A distinguished panel of guests would judge the event. The panel for the first Danbury Cup in October 1975 included the President of the Society, and later long-term member of the Danbury chapter, Dick Ellenberger.[20] In that initial contest, between the Nashua, New Hampshire, chapter and the Danbury chapter, all five of the top quartets were from Danbury: "Over the Hill" Mob, Connecticut Chord Company, Random Sample, Last Call, and Final Decision.[21]

The purpose of the activity was to encourage quartet singing. It also supported Tony Grosz's vision of a chapter that was comprised of quartets, rather than of a chorus whose members occasionally formed quartets. Since there could be no "repeats"—in other words, no one could sing in more than one quartet—the Danbury chapter had an advantage in these contests, since they had grown by that time to more than eighty members and could therefore simply field more talented quartets than other choruses. However, there were circumstances in which the visiting team won the cup.[22]

In the fall of 1974, the Danbury chapter's successes continued. They did not improve on their 1973 finish in the district contest, but only because of an eight-point deduction from the arrangement judges due to the daring nature of their music. In the quartet competition, the Lavender Hill Mob reached the pinnacle of its competitive success. In the summer of 1974, lead John Ahearn was forced to quit the quartet due to business

2.3 *(opposite) Last Call*

obligations and was replaced by Poughkeepsie lead Mike Myers. This only improved the sound of an already excellent quartet. Tony Grosz recalled one rehearsal at tenor Ray Wixted's home on Danbury's South Street with a coach from the area in preparation for that district contest. The Lavender Hill Mob was preparing two Irish-themed songs in that coaching session: "Young Roddy McCorley," about the Irish rebellion of 1798, and "Tumble Down Shack in Athlone." In completing the set, Grosz, who would later have a spiritual experience that would set him off on a life of exploring consciousness, remembers the moment as his most transcendental experience in music. "It was as if time had stopped," Grosz recalls, "and everyone in the room was in that tumble down shack together." When

the song finally finished, the coach in the room was crying. His advice was simply: "Do that on the stage."[23]

At the Boston Districts in 1974, the quality of Lavender Hill Mob's performance was as sublime as it had been in practice. When the contest was won by the Four-N-Aires from the Saratoga Springs chapter, there was an audible gasp of surprise, and for some, disappointment in in Boston at that result, as the audience appeared to expect the Lavender Hill Mob to win.[24] They finished a close second in that contest, the best result of any Danbury chapter quartet ever.[25]

1975 continued this competitive and performance success for the Mad Hatters, albeit with some changes. The Lavender Hill Mob disbanded, as Tony Grosz and Mike Myers joined with two other Poughkeepsie men, Fred Gielow, baritone, and Pete Donatelli, tenor, to form The Brotherhood, a very popular group that performed across the United States and Canada in the late 1970s. Danbury continued to improve, moving up to eighth in the District, two spots behind Poughkeepsie and second in Connecticut behind the then-powerful Housatonic-Derby chapter.[26]

The Danbury group also put on a memorable Annual Show in that year, "Hats Off to History," at Danbury High School. It celebrated old-time music with dueling banjos played by Joy Coughlin and bass singer Clark Coughlin. The 1975 program also introduced the Mad Hatter Rascals, a comedy-oriented "Very Large Quartet" featuring the antics of the popular "Lonesome Joe" Talarico, as well as performance from the Connecticut Chord Company, featuring Jack Williams, Jack Deane, Gene Buck, and Bill Manion; the Last Call with Bob Stewart, Jack Tyler, Mario Merolle, and Len Carlson; the Random Sample with Jack Foley, Bob Smith, Jr, Ray Waldron, and Ron Meade, and the Lavender Hill Mob in what was perhaps their final performance.

By mid-1975, the ranks of the chorus had swelled to ninety-two men. 1975 was a banner year for the chorus's public service mission as well. The chorus sang for convicts interned at the Hartford County Jail and at the

2.4 *(opposite) The Brotherhood at the 1977 International Convention*

Federal Correctional Institute in Danbury. This proved, as baritone Bill Cooley from Monroe quipped, "there's nothing like a captive audience."[27]

Of the fifty long years of the Danbury Mad Hatter Chorus, there is little doubt that 1976 was the most eventful year, and possibly the Mad Hatters' most significant turning point. The event that galvanized the chorus and reverberated across the many years to come was the decision of the Board of Directors to force the Director of the Chorus, Tony Grosz, to resign over disagreements about whether the Board or the Director had creative control over repertoire.

On its surface, the decision to remove Grosz seems shocking. In fact, tension between the Director and the Board began as early as late 1975. It appears to have originally arisen over contest qualifications. Attached to the July 1975 minutes was a letter to the director from President Gerry Otton on behalf of the board in regard to contest qualifications. The letter

was a follow-up from a previous clash between members of the board and Grosz about how fast to advance singing quality, and it reads as the board's capitulation to the Director on this issue. "Your talents," the board letter reads, "have not been fully utilized because the chapter goals for singing quality have not been set high enough by the board."[28] The board's letter, therefore, was designed to give Grosz the ability to implement more stringent qualifications for contests and sing-outs.[29]

However, an additional purpose of the letter was to remind Grosz that these decisions should be made by the Music Committee, rather than solely by him, and that the system of qualifications should include some system of instruction that would allow members who were struggling to qualify to improve their craft. "The need for this program," in which "the director will allow every man to learn," according to the President, was "urgent." And this learning should come not only from the director, but also from "the assistant directors, section leaders, and knowledgeable members." The director was charged with creating such a plan quickly so that the Board could consider it at their August 1975 meeting.

On July 29, 1975, Tony Grosz responded with a Contest Preparation Plan that included a scheme to create individual coaching sessions for members with the Music Committee rather than holding twice-a-week rehearsals, and to qualify members while the chorus, as a whole, was performing rather than through listening to members in quartets and octets. In the letter, he thanked the Board for assuring him of their "backing" and acknowledged that he served as Director "at the will of the board." However, notably, it is clear that this plan was not made in consultation with the Music Committee or at a Music Committee meeting, as specified by the board.[30] In Grosz's reply, there was a hint of some of the bombast that members recall from him at the time. At one meeting in the fall of 1975, Grosz made an impassioned speech to the membership to the effect that if they wanted him to be their director, they had to do things his way.[31] The exchange of letters appears not to have been the end of the qualification issue. At their October 1975 meeting, the board decided that every chorus member who had signed up for the Montreal district contest would go and would sing, seemingly contravening the qualification requirements set up by Grosz.[32]

The issue over qualifications may have increased tensions between Grosz and the board, but there was no open animosity. At the May 1976 meeting, for example, the Chapter agreed to donate $150 to the Brotherhood quartet to defray their costs to compete at the International competition in San Francisco that year (where they placed 39th), despite the fact that Tony Grosz was the only chapter member in the quartet. Yet at that same meeting "there was an extensive discussion as to the directorship and the chorus goals for the coming year by the board," which was deemed important enough to discuss with the chorus as a whole at the next rehearsal.[33] The minutes do not discuss the details of the disagreement, though it is clear that it was about Grosz's music selections for the upcoming show. The problem, apparently, was not so much with the quality of the music being chosen. Instead, the members of the board felt that music was being selected without proper input from the board, the chorus as a whole, or even the music committee.[34] The issue may also have been to some extent about Grosz's occasionally confrontational personality. Grosz demanded respect. When the chorus was performing at a Catholic church, he once—jokingly—pointed up to Jesus on the Crucifix and said, "that's what happened to the last person who didn't follow the director!"[35] While this was meant in jest, the point behind it must have been lost on no one.

As a result, at the Board Meeting on June 3, 1976, Dick Bristol, the long-time secretary of the Mad Hatters, made a motion that Grosz "be dismissed as director of the chorus." This motion was defeated by a margin of 3 to 5. John Perkins, the Vice President for Administration, then made a motion that the Board communicate to Grosz within two days a request that he resign, and terminate him if he did not agree to resign. That motion carried by a vote of 7 to 1. Perkins then moved that Ray Wixted be made interim director, with the understanding that there would be a search for a permanent director at a later date, and that motion carried unanimously.[36] Wixted would eventually become that permanent director, and would stay on for eleven years until his own resignation in November 1987.

In hindsight, the Board's decision was a terrible mistake. It is easy to understand both sides of this dispute. The Danbury chorus had a proud tradition of Board control, a tradition that was then, and is now, written in to the Society's operating standards for chapters. Unlike in some classical settings, the music director of a barbershop chorus is not the *maestro*, whose creative control is beyond question. In its early years, the Danbury chorus was extremely board-centered, even to the point to which the music director in the 1960s was almost an afterthought in board minutes and in publicity.[37] This trend only began to change in 1970, after the chorus began losing members and attendance because of poor singing and Bill Manion began to assert more aggressive leadership; but even in that case, Manion proved to be a very deferential leader, and arrived at sing-out standards at the request of the board, and in collaboration with the music committee. Clearly, the board had a right to object to Grosz's occasionally director-centric leadership style.

On the other hand, the effectiveness of that leadership style cannot be disputed. In the short years of Grosz's tenure, the chorus went from a membership of thirty-eight to at least ninety-two. Though the improvement in the chorus's contest results began under Bill Manion's direction, they improved exponentially under Grosz. The Mad Hatters went from one that was consistently near the bottom of the division to one that was competing at the top of the district. Both the chorus's increase in membership and quality can be attributed to Grosz personally. In fact, ironically, both can be attributed to the very decision making for which the board dismissed him. Ray Waldron, who was on the Board at the time of Grosz's dismissal, had himself said in 1975 that the chapter's growth could be attributed to the fact that "the better singer" was "enticed by the quality of our barbershop-style song repertoire," a repertoire that Waldron attributed to Grosz personally: "Tony's hard work and insistence on quality helps to keep the good singer interested."[38]

When asked about what caused the sharp spike in membership and contest scores in this period, Bob Connolley (b. 1925), who joined the chorus in November 1972, and was chosen as Barbershopper of the Quarter in the summer of 1976, at the time of Tony Grosz's dismissal, said bluntly: "Tony Gross was a good director. He made things lots of fun and made sure there was good singing."[39] It was not just that the chapter doubled in size; it was also that the legions of new members were among the best singers in the chapter.

The greatest achievements of the chorus were made not under the leadership of Tony Grosz, but under that of his successor, Ray Wixted. It was under Wixted, not Grosz, that the chorus reached its greatest competitive success, placing fifth in the district in 1977 and again in 1981, and being crowned division champions in 1980 and 1982. Though the exact date is not entirely clear, it is likely that the chorus's high water mark in membership, 99 members, was achieved in late 1976 under Wixted, not under Grosz. This was a moment that many former members remember as a highlight; Bob Connolley specifically remembers that the moment that the ninety-ninth member was announced at a chapter meeting, longtime secretary Dick Bristol proclaimed that he was going to go out onto Main Street in Danbury and stop a school bus if that was what was necessary to get to 100 members. Unfortunately, the Danbury chapter never made it to 100.[40]

This version is only the most popular of the many stories that go with the lore of the elusive hundredth member. Former chapter president Jack Cramer (b. 1941) remembers another version of the story. In this iteration, Bristol proclaimed that he was going to troll the alleys of Danbury with a wine bottle until he found someone he could coerce into being the hundredth man.[41] When asked about the discrepancy, Cramer observed that both stories might well be true. Longtime member Bob Stewart remembers driving back from a contest in Montreal in the 1980s and having the car, which was driven by Dick Bristol, stopped at the border. When the Border Patrol officer asked him whether he had left anything in Canada, he answered, to the uproarious laughter of the guard and his singing mates in the car: "just a few stools."[42]

Though Bristol was certainly at the center of the movement to dismiss Grosz, he also exemplified the light-hearted spirit that was fostered under Grosz's leadership. Jack Cramer recalls that Grosz was "humorous in a professorial way." His light-heartedness allowed him to control the chorus which had a mix of strong personalities and, in Cramer's words, the kind of "big egos" that often come with a group of good singers. In particular, taming the "booming voice" of Joe Talarico without "upsetting his stature" was a skill that only Tony Grosz possessed. He managed to encourage the humor of the clowns in the chapter such as Mario Merolle, Jack Foley, and Bob Stewart (who once famously mooned his illustrious director while traveling down Main Street in Danbury) without having their antics become a distraction in rehearsals. With the chorus growing at a blistering pace and more egos being brought into the mix, perhaps, as Cramer speculates, the clash of personalities proved more than even the very talented Grosz could handle.[43]

There can be no doubt that Wixted deserves considerable credit for the accomplishments of the Mad Hatters in the 1970s and early 1980s. He was by all accounts an energetic and capable director. He was a consummate teacher who was good at setting goals and implementing a vision for the chorus. That being said, these results were an after-effect of the size and might of the Danbury chapter that was built, more than by anyone else, by Tony Grosz. By the early 1980s, the chapter began a slow decline that lasted for more than twenty years. Its membership rolls were never again nearly as large, and its performance success has never again matched that achieved from the mid-1970s to the early 1980s. Given these facts, one could make an argument that the decision to terminate Tony Grosz was, in fact, a decision from which the chorus has never recovered. In the words of Bob Connolley, the reason for the decline of the chapter was that it "lost a good director." As Connolley notes, while "Ray did a great job for us for quite some time," it is nevertheless the case that the chorus "went slowly downhill after losing Tony Grosz."[44]

Today, Anton Grosz, who no longer seems to refer to himself as "Tony," recalls little of the terms of the dispute that caused his departure from the Danbury chapter. He, perhaps graciously, chooses not to speak of it, and remembers that there were also other factors that caused him to be willing to leave directing in Danbury. The long commute from Poughkeepsie, rain or shine, was hard on him and his family. In what may have been a harbinger of things to come, on one rainy night, Grosz was traveling down Interstate 84 in Putnam County, New York, after midnight following the culmination of a long rehearsal. Grosz passed a car going full speed in the wrong direction on the highway, and he came to the sudden realization that, had he been in a different lane, that moment would have been his last.[45]

In 1978, Anton Grosz had a spiritual experience that led him to commit the rest of his life to comprehending consciousness and returning-from-death experiences. He has researched the *Bardo Thodol* extensively. Colloquially known as the "Tibetan Book of the Dead," this work is a text from the Nyigma tradition of Vajrayana (Tibetan) Buddhism, and is about the enlightenment that is possible from becoming conscious of the intermediate state between two existences. His major publication on these subjects, *Letters to a Dying Friend*, features a preface written by the Dalai Lama. It was inspired by the sudden and unexpected death of his Brotherhood quartet mate, Pete Donatelli, of a massive heart attack while jogging with his German shepherd in 1984.[46]

Inspired by spiritual experiences, Grosz quit singing barbershop entirely in 1980 to spend time on more important matters. He moved to California in 1989, earned a Doctoral degree in Philosophy and Religion from the California Institute of Integral Studies in 1995, and has worked as a Spiritual and Bereavement Counselor for Crossroads Home Care and Hospice in San Francisco ever since.

Meanwhile, after the dismissal of Tony Grosz, the chorus still had their greatest accomplishments ahead of them. In 1977, a newly invigorated music committee, in consultation with Ray Wixted and the board, decided that the chapter was going to have two musical goals. The first was to "advance the performing skills of our chorus to the level of District Champion and International contender." The second was to "provide to the Danbury area a musical organization whose quality of performance and professionalism is second to none."[47] In the short term, in the year 1977, the music team hoped to win the division championship and come home from the district contest with "at least a fifth place ribbon."[48] These short-term goals, while ambitious, were not impossible: in the October 1976 district contest in Portland, Maine, Danbury placed ninth, but only thirteen points separated them and the sixth-place Nashua, New Hampshire, chapter. In the Division Contest in 1976, the Mad Hatters were second only to the Housatonic-Derby chapter, but the score differential was almost fifty points, making the goal of winning division, in a way, the more difficult one.

Wixted and the music team realized that these long-term goals would require a major commitment on the part of the Mad Hatters. "Our top priority will be given to this endeavor," they made clear on their goals list, referring to the implementation of a stricter qualifications system, the type of which Grosz had tried, and apparently failed, to achieve in 1975. The music team fully realized that insisting on good singing "could possibly mean the reduction of the performance chorus to as few as 35 men," but that was a risk they were willing to take for excellence in competition results. The music committee would "teach to the faster elements of the chorus," would bring in more outside coaching, and would ensure at least thirty minutes of weekly sectionals.[49] In their letter to the members of the chapter, the music team asserted "not all members share this goal with us and do not wish to make the effort required. We accept this and welcome these individuals to stay with us," on the understanding that "they will not be part of the performing chorus at major singing events."[50]

In early 1977, the Mad Hatters were not yet ready to realize those goals. At the division contest, the Mad Hatters closed the gap between themselves and the Derby chapter to thirty-two points, but they still came in second. The problems in the performance were ones that the Mad Hatters struggled with in the past and are still challenged by in the present: section unity in the lead section, a few synchronization errors, and a lack of presence in the tenor section. Still, the arrangement judge noted that the chorus sound was the cleanest he had heard in quite some time.[51]

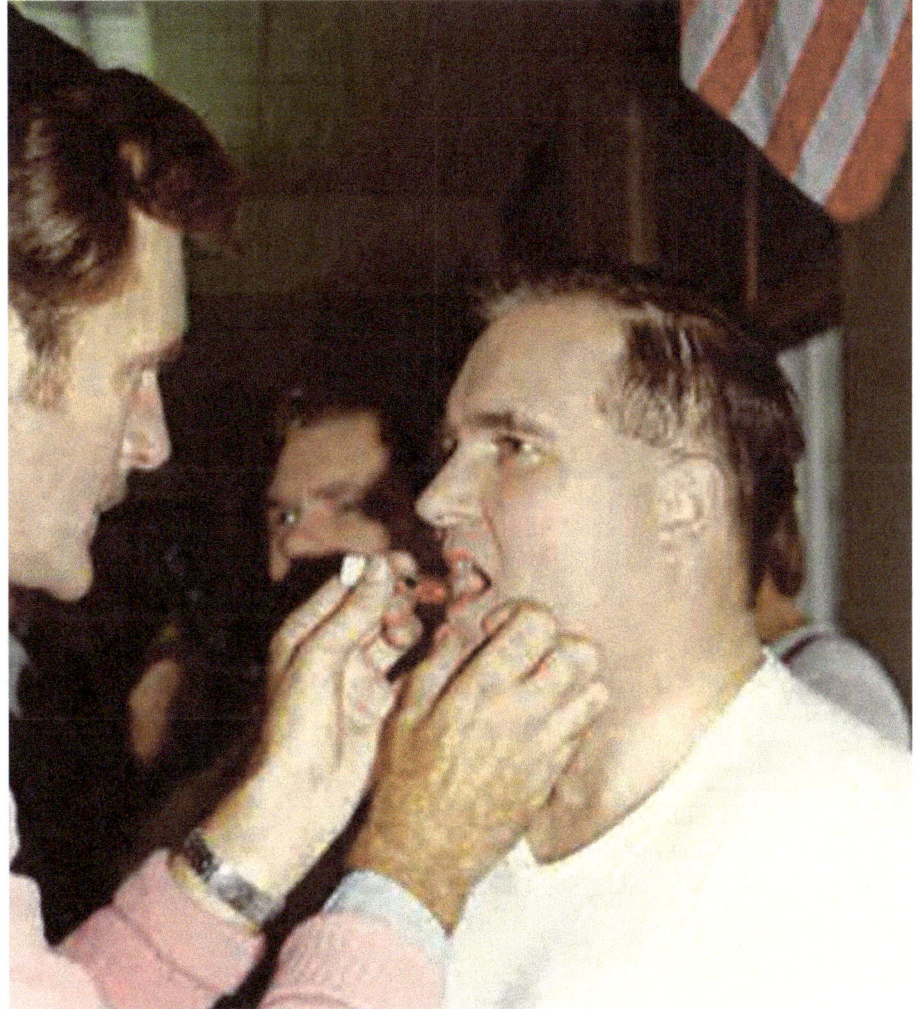

2.5 *Preparing makeup for the 1977 District Contest*

The chorus walked away from that contest knowing one problem would be resolved: the perennial complaints about the lack of good uniforms. In January 1977, the Board voted to purchase black tuxedos with white piping used from the Dallas Tidelanders Chorus at the cost (quite considerable for that era) of $42.00 each, to be implemented as the chorus uniform by April 15, 1977. Insofar as the chorus lost several points on uniforms at division, that problem would be solved at the 1977 district contest.

By the District Contest in Lake Placid, New York, on October 22, 1977, the Mad Hatters, with fifty-five members on stage, reached their goal, placing fifth with a total score of 736 points.[52] The October/November 1977 edition of the Mad Hatter newsletter, the *Hatter Chatter*, gushed:

> Man Alive! We're number five! Maybe by the skin of our teeth, we won that glorious green ribbon (by 8 points), but win it we did, and now we know, there's only one way to go, and that's up, up, and up to 1st Place!!!!!! Can we do it? YOU BETCHA!!!!!!!!! And maybe we didn't generate some excitement in that huge auditorium when the announcement was made! Our reaction, jubilation, and joy, was greater than those who did better, and that's GREAT!!!!!![53]

Achieving the fifth place ribbon was a vindication of the aggressive qualification strategy of Ray Wixted and the music committee. To this day, some members of the Mad Hatters remember this moment, along with the fifth place finish in 1981, as one of the main highlights of their time with the chorus.[54] This strategy was not without its risks. The competition success corresponded with a waning in active attendance and a decline in membership. From a peak membership of ninety-nine in 1976, the Mad Hatters fell to eighty members by December 1977. A survey of member activity in the fourth quarter of 1977 revealed 56 active members (those attending more than 50% of events), 5 semi-active members (those attending 25–50% of events), 8 temporarily inactive members (those attending less that 25% of events) and 11 permanently inactive members (those who had attended no events).[55] It seems, in other words, that the stringent qualifications had made the contest chorus the *de facto* chorus—it had, in fact, reduced the chapter from more than eighty active members to just fifty-six.

During this era, the Mad Hatters continued to have an extraordinary cast of characters in their chapter. Frank Golden (1916–2008), a famous artist who was the main illustrator for *Sports Illustrated* in the 1960s and 1970s and who painted the background of Salvador Dali's *The Dream of Venus* for the 1939 World's Fair, was a member in these years, and he designed the evocative shoulder patches that were the trademarks of the chorus for many years.[56] Several Mad Hatters were fine musicians: Bill Manion, John LaBosco, and Ray Wixted played piano; Len Carlson played tuba; several members played the guitar; Gordon Finch was a local elementary school music teacher who also played the cornet.

A number of the Mad Hatters in that era were veterans of World War II, the Korean War, or the Vietnam War, and gained experience in singing while in the military. Burt Rosendahl, who had the speaking voice of a radio announcer, flew combat missions over Germany in World War II (in the same squadron as Jimmy Stewart); he also sang with a "small group of GIs in England." Several other veterans rounded out an extraordinary group of pilots who sang with the group in the 1970s and 1980s. Jim Bradley and Ed Harvey were both fighter pilots in the Vietnam War. Harvey and John Tenaglia both flew commercially for Trans World Airlines, while Dick Beckner and Dan Duda both flew for United. Part of the character of the chorus in those years—along with the good singing—can be attributed to the rapidity with which the chorus added doo-wop singers to their ranks. Bob Stanczak, Larry Angeli, Mario Merolle, and Bob Stewart had all been doo-wop singers in their prime, and even today, Stewart sings doo-wop with the Uptown Express, a popular doo-wop group in Florida.[57]

Despite the decrease in overall chapter size, Wixted kept this still very large and occasionally undisciplined chorus focused. He hailed from Danbury and was from a musical family. He received musical training from his mother, Marion Durkin Wixted, who was herself a classically trained vocalist. At Danbury High School in the 1950s, he became the leader of the Ray Wixted Band, through which he met his high school sweetheart and future wife Carolyn. Though not formally educated in music, Wixted held a number of musical positions throughout his life, including being the Choir Director of the Saint Gregory the Great Church in Danbury, as well as its organist, for more than thirty years. He was also a consummate teacher who inspired history and social studies students at New Fairfield High for decades. Wixted regarded directing a choir and teaching history as two fundamentally similar teaching opportunities, since teaching was just a way of "giving five performances a day." He was, more than anything, a "ham," an occasionally goofy teacher who could give the Mad Hatters the spirit they needed.[58]

The 1977 and 1978 shows also provided a high point of the chorus in this era. They featured a new generation of quartets, including a relatively short-lived but apparently excellent group with the memorable name "The Great Eastern Union Singing Telegram Company," featuring Jack Williams on tenor, Ray Wixted on lead, Dick Hess on baritone, and Len Carlson on bass. This era also saw the emergence of a quartet that was locally popular throughout the late 1970s: Cold Water Flat, featuring Larry Angeli on tenor, Bob Stewart on lead, Gene Buck on baritone, and Dick Zang on bass.[59]

In 1978, the Mad Hatters continued their competitive success, though the results require closer analysis to see it. In the division contest, the Mad Hatters placed a disappointing fourth, not only behind Housatonic-Derby, which took their usual place on top, but also behind two surging chapters in Manchester and New London. However, the Mad Hatters scored a 372, an eight-point improvement over their 1977 district score, and achieved their best score ever in the stage presence category.

Despite these competitive successes, membership continued to decline and attendance at meetings suffered. By May 1978, the total chapter membership declined to seventy-four. Attendance was down 11.2% in

2.6 *(opposite) Final Decision*

comparison to a year before; an average of twelve fewer members attended meetings than the previous year. In response, an ad hoc committee on membership was formed which tried to answer the question of why membership was "hard to come by."

In an extensive report, the committee concluded that the chapter meetings were no longer as much fun because they did not present challenges; that members were not able to air their grievances with the board and have questions answered; that the Hatter Chatter should be mailed to the home addresses of all members; that the chorus should not intimidate or throw out members who chose to hang out in the Rathskeller

Bar during chapter meetings, but should rather make the meetings interesting enough to entice members to leave their beers and come sing; that more inclusive opportunities to sing should be made at the Rathskeller; and that more bars should be visited. More importantly, the committee felt that more exciting and better-organized sing-outs would be a key to restoring flagging attendance.[60]

These grievances revealed a morale problem lurking behind the competitive success, which was of sufficient concern that, in the course of comments to the Board on the desirability of using "Alexander's Ragtime Band" as a contest tune for the District Contest in Burlington, Vermont, in the fall of 1978, Ray Wixted said that "he feels a more positive attitude is necessary if the chorus is to win in Burlington."[61] As a result of the grievances of the *ad hoc* committee, the Mad Hatters engaged in several exciting sing-outs. In September 1978, they held a show at the Statler-Hilton Hotel in New York for a meeting of the Supreme Emblem Club of the United States of America, the unofficial female auxiliary of the Elks Club. In that gig, the Mad Hatters performed to an audience estimated at more than 1200 people, and pulled off a wonderful show including the debut of the "Girl Package" featuring the songs "Give Me A Girl" and "For Me and My Gal."[62] They also held an exciting interchapter with the Nashua, New Hampshire, chorus.

In March 1979, the Mad Hatters continued to focus on solving their declining membership problem by holding an open house for men interested in barbershop. By that time, the average attendance at rehearsals had declined to forty-three.[63] The open house did appear to net two new members, but that was not enough to halt the larger trend. The highlight of the year was "Girls, Girls, Girls," the Chapter's annual show, featuring a reworked Girl Set including "Give Me A Girl," and "The Girl in My Memory." The show also featured the Nashua chapter as a guest, along with a comedy quartet from Canton, Massachusetts, the Blue Hill Four. What was most memorable, however, was a performance by the Boston Common at the show, who were at the height of their popularity in the

Northeast in that era and would go on to win the gold medal at International in 1980, the next year.[64]

In the spring of 1980, the Mad Hatters achieved another first, winning the division contest in March in Pittsfield, Massachusetts. By the summer of 1980, the chorus had turned its attention away from competition, at least to some extent, to turn all of its focus to the problem of waning interest and declining membership. The drive for competitive success was really taking its toll. Declining membership was more than merely a morale problem. It was also a financial burden on the chapter's plans. Because the Mad Hatters were funded with a combination of package shows, dues and raffles, the smaller the chapter was, the fewer the activities would be in which the members could participate. In the January 1980 Board Meeting, someone pointed out that Ray Wixted had been appointed only as an interim director in 1976, and that a search for a new permanent director had been pursued in 1976 and 1977 and then abandoned. When approached about this, the Chapter President, Frank Ferrito, explained that the search had been abandoned because of the financial problems of the chapter.[65]

Morale had been further lowered back in 1979 when the Elks Club began charging the chapter a substantial rent. As a result, chorus members retaliated by boycotting the Rathskeller Bar, whose best clients had been the notoriously boozy members of the Mad Hatters. In 1980, this boycott was lifted because it "simply was not effective."[66] But in the meantime, the boycott must have reduced morale. The Rathskeller had been the center of informal quartetting and singing activity since the meetings had been moved to the Elks Club from the Danbury Motor Inn back in late 1967, and a great deal of the "fun" to be had with the chorus had been tied with the imbibing of alcoholic beverages. The boycott was also not very effective because members were not adhering to it. Simultaneously with the boycott arose the problem of Chapter members drinking heavily before the start of rehearsal. The Board considered disallowing the practice, but settled for discouraging it.[67] As the *ad hoc* committee had previously noted, however, the fact that members were more interested in drinking than in meetings may have shown that something was wrong with the rehearsals.

To address this problem, membership chairman Jack Cramer worked to make communications between the board and the membership more transparent, to reinstitute more backyard gatherings and the annual clambake, and to hold a guest night in which the chapter pulled out the stops. These efforts seem to have been temporarily successful in stanching the tide of defections. By May 1980, membership had risen to sixty-nine, and the April guest night yielded forty guests, among which five likely members were to be culled.

Having stabilized the membership situation, by September 1980 the chorus shifted its focus back to excellence in contests. In the midst of the financial and membership crises, the music committee had become moribund and had to be re-formed. In November 1980, a committee composed of Frank Ferrito, Ray Wixted, Bill Manion, and Dick Zang met and sketched out a proposed new structure for an expanded and deliberative music committee, which was then adopted by the chorus.[68]

At their January 1981 meeting, the music committee set two related goals: winning their division and getting back into the top five at the district contest. A third goal was to create a demonstrable improvement in vowel production, breathing, and consistency of performance. The Music Committee implemented a clearer, more integrated rehearsal schedule and increased the rapidity with which songs were to be learned.[69] They then planned an extensive combination of coaching, including visits from Poughkeepsie standout Steve Plumb and noted arranger and director Renee Craig. By the summer, they had chosen to sing the new "Rosie" set for the competition, with the songs "Meet Me in Rosetime Rose," and "Midnight Rose."[70] These efforts paid off. Although the Mad Hatters did not win the division championship in 1981, they went back to Lake Placid and placed fifth, matching their best result, previously achieved in 1977. The Mad Hatters were again singing at their highest level, and were holding their membership together.

The renewed focus on musical excellence emanating from a new, collaborative, and larger music committee had effects that were felt into 1982. Perhaps the most successful contest in Mad Hatters history was the Division contest held in Warwick, Rhode Island, in March 1982. Again singing the Rosie set, the Mad Hatters were crowned the best in the division—which at the time also encompassed the State of Connecticut—in a still-crowded field with eleven other barbershop choruses. Moreover, 1982 was a great year for chapter quartets. Several well-known chapter quartets had their coming of age in the 1982 division contest. Harmony Accord, featuring Frank Golden (tenor), Stan Rushton (lead), Jack Spenard (baritone) and Bill Keenan (bass), won the Novice Championship, while Summertime, featuring Jack Foley (tenor), Bob Stewart (lead), Mike McFarlane (baritone) and Len Carlson (bass), won

2.7 *Chorus President Bob Smith pins the Director's Award on Director Ray Wixted, District Contest, 1981*

the Division Championship. Right behind them, however, was another Danbury quartet in second place: Nutmeg Heritage, featuring Ray Wixted (tenor), Hal Kolp (lead), George King (baritone) and Bob Allen (bass).[71]

The 1982 success was the result of a doubling down on an expanded music committee. In 1982, this committee had ten members and was chaired by Bill Manion. It had a budget of $1,615, which paid for two scholarships to Harmony College (now Harmony University), coaching sessions, choreography sessions, and music. The expanded budget allowed the music committee to bring in more coaching, and because the committee was inclusive, it generated less resentment and misunderstanding than had characterized the 1977–1978 efforts, which focused more heavily on qualifying or disqualifying members than it did on coaching or repertoire. Interestingly, however, the 1982 goals for the chapter did not include repeating the fifth place performance at Districts. Rather, they focused on more abstract potential achievements, such as improving "as a competitive chorus," putting on a "musically successful show," and increasing "the quality and quantity of quartet activity."[72] Despite these vague goals, however, the music committee continued to innovate, producing a very organized program on craft, with each member of the committee taking charge of one aspect of craft for the rehearsals.[73] After years of discussion, 1982 was the year that the Mad Hatters first started ensuring that all members received audiotapes containing learning tracks of the entire chorus repertoire.[74]

The result was that in 1982 the Mad Hatters were at the top of the charts for the Northeast District's Plateau 5 in what the Society at the time called Achievement (formerly Protention)—which was a combined measure of a chorus's performance and retention. They had gained ten members since the beginning of 1981 and performed well in contest, and that was good for fourteenth place in the society in the Achievement category.[75]

Despite not repeating the ribbon-winning performance at Districts, 1982 was a good year for the Mad Hatter chorus. In the words of President

2.8 *Summertime*

Jack Cramer, "our average meeting attendance is up, we have improved our singing ability, we had three very competitive quartets in action, we strengthened our financial position and we have organized a bevy of fine people to ensure our continued success."[76]

Unfortunately, 1982 was to be the last truly good year for the Mad Hatters in the twentieth century. For the rest of the 1980s, the quality of the Mad Hatters' singing gradually deteriorated, which led by the late 1980s and early 1990s to a precipitous decline in membership. 1983 started promisingly enough. An invigorated music committee was ensuring that the chorus would receive regular coaching from Society standout and Westchester Chordsmen director Renee Craig and had also purchased two arrangements from her.

There were, however, two signs of trouble. The first was a memo to Ray Wixted as Director and Bill Manion as Music Committee Chairman from President Jack Cramer. The memo indicated that "the format and all programming of regular chapter meetings" should be "the direct responsibility of the music committee." This directive emerged from Cramer's perception that as of March 15, 1983, too much time had been spent on fun items and that the chorus was not prepared going into the May 7th Division contest.[77]

The second item of concern was another memo from Cramer to Bill Manion expressing dismay at the lack of planning and preparation for the annual show and the fall division contest. Cramer was worried because he was not aware of a fall coaching schedule in preparation for competition, of any choreography and riser position plans for the fall, of any preparation schedule for the fall, or of the planned music for division in spring 1984. He was not even sure what the current repertoire was.[78]

In his reply, Bill Manion said that Cramer had failed to read the July 1983 minutes of the Music Committee, which would answer his questions, and set his mind at ease that the chorus was in the "best shape" that "we have ever been in."[79] Nevertheless, Cramer's concerns reflected an anxiety

2.9 (opposite) Bob Connolley enjoying the annual clambake, 1978

that despite the efforts of the highly organized Music Committee, the chorus might not have been headed in the right direction.

Notwithstanding these concerns, morale remained high in 1983. The chapter quartets were still enjoying considerable success, buoying the spirits of the rest of the chorus. Nutmeg Heritage came out on top of the 1983 division contest. They were to go on to place a respectable twenty-fourth in the district contest.[80] The summer backyard sing-outs continued unabated. Joe Talarico's backyard sing-out generated a huge crowd that year—more than usual even for him—and singing went on for hours as friends, neighbors, and guests enjoyed the famous sausages and corn for which this event had become known. The summer also featured a backyard sing-out sponsored by Paul Kennedy and a successful annual picnic. Even as singing began to slide, for the moment, membership was stable and morale was as good as ever.[81]

At the district competition, which was held in Providence, Rhode Island, in October 1983, the Mad Hatters placed eighth, which was still a

very good finish, but clearly indicative of a decrease in musical quality. The Danbury chapter still fielded a very respectable fifty-three men on the risers to sing "Maggie" and "Roll on Mississippi." The chorus was praised for putting out a solid sound, and for easily producing expanded sound and overtones. However, perhaps as a result of the easing of the hardline chorus qualifications of the late 1970s over concerns about fleeing membership, the judges found that the performance was just a little sloppy. The basses were not holding vowel sounds, individual basses and tenors could be heard going flat, volume changes were too sudden, and competitors were watching the judges rather than the director. The performance needed "fine tuning."[82]

While President Jack Cramer was first to see the writing on the wall indicating that the chorus was in a slow decline, the Board of Directors quickly caught on. In the last board meeting of 1983, the Board held a discussion "relative to the music, and the Music Committee. Music is, of course, a major concern of the Board of Directors. The Music Committee needs revitalization, and this should be a priority of the board. Discussion was also undertaken relative to assistant directors."[83]

While the Board may have been concerned about the decline of the quality of singing, they failed to make this aspect a major goal for the chapter in 1984. Instead, they focused on improving "the rate of learning and introduction of new music," an important but tangential issue to the quality of singing, and on significantly increasing "community awareness of our organization." This second goal might improve membership, but only if the community were interested in the product the chorus was offering.[84]

Despite this, the Board and the Music Committee attempted to address the decline of singing by initiating the RISE (Rapid Improvement in Singing Excellence) program, which was a program designed to coach individual members on the 1984 contest set. That set consisted of "Hello My Baby" and "Somebody's Coming to Town." The RISE program asked each section leader to sing "unison duets" with each member of the chorus to check for note and word problems, in the belief that this would "improve our contest scores, show quality and overall barbershop fun in a very short time span."[85] In addition, the Music Committee budget was increased to $2,160 to cover more coaching and scholarships to Society educational events.[86] In the Spring of 1984, four extra rehearsals were scheduled and a staging plan with a "college theme" to link the songs together was devised.[87] Despite these efforts, however, at the District Contest in Worcester, Massachusetts, in 1984, the chorus placed ninth. This was still a good finish, but it was indicative of a stagnating chorus.

For the first half of 1985, the chorus appears to have gotten sidetracked on two issues far afield from singing. The first was growing discontent with the rehearsal facilities at the Elks Lodge, which had begun several years earlier when the Elks began to charge rent. By 1985, the facilities were showing their age and were approaching a state of disrepair. However, committees looking into the issue had difficulties finding an alternate venue in the area of downtown Danbury that would meet the requirements of the chorus.[88] The second issue was preparing for the annual show. The chorus renewed its focus on having a good show in 1985, which was to be held at Danbury High School on November 23rd, in order to make money and recruit new members. They re-booked the New Jersey comedy quartet the Note-Wits in the hopes that they would draw a large crowd.[89]

These issues distracted the Board of Directors and the Music Committee. They were not able to focus on stopping the slow decline in the quality of music performance. While the Music Committee did approve perennial Mad Hatter favorite "On the Sunny Side of the Street" as well as "Where Have All My Friends Gone" as the contest package and booked coaching with the very capable Steve Plumb, the Music Committee still needed to be urged, almost into the summer, to reinstitute the RISE program. The Committee seems to have been preoccupied by the distribution of learning tapes. Predictably, scores suffered. Since winning the division in 1980 and 1982, the Mad Hatters had returned to an age-old pattern of coming in second to the then-powerful Valley Chordsmen of the Waterbury-Derby chapter. But in 1985, the Manchester Chorus surpassed them for second as well.[90] In the District Competition, which was held in Montreal, Quebec, the Danbury men came in eleventh.[91] In the aftermath of the contest, the board concluded the following:

> The contest result may have short changed Danbury as indicated by widely differing scoring by judges in sound, stage presence, and interpretation categories. Use of the more favorable scores would have placed us 5th, rather than 11th. Still, as [Chapter President Paul] Kennedy pointed out and acknowledged by the board present, Danbury has not programmed the type of training necessary to correcting our major weakness in the sound category. We receive excellent coaching, as at the TV camp weekend, but then fail to build on it. The Green Book is available as a training tool, but we do not use it. Kennedy, and selected board members, will meet with the Music Committee to present the Board's concerns and recommendations for corrective actions.[92]

What Kennedy, the Music Committee, and the Board decided was to try to spur action from the Music Committee by appointing former SPEB-SQSA President Dick Ellenberger as Music Committee Chair for 1986, with the understanding that he would be much more active in forcing change.

After a meeting with one another, Wixted and Ellenberger decided that the right approach was a return to fundamentals. They advocated a return to the "Rosie Package," with which the chorus had reached the height of their scoring, featuring "Midnight Rose" and "Meet Me in Rosetime Rose," with the hopes that familiar songs that had scored well would allow the chorus to focus on technique. They then booked a series of coaching sessions with Renee Craig, who "took an old music package and made it new."[93] This seemed like a solid idea, but it did not work. At division in Manchester, Connecticut, in March 1986, Danbury placed fourth, now having been overtaken by Waterbury-Derby, Manchester, and Meriden. The Rosie set was too stale to motivate the chorus, and too many engrained habits could not be broken. Prior to the contest, the Music Committee had held an unscheduled meeting to consider reversing themselves and inserting a new "Rosie" song as had been previously contemplated, but it was too late.[94]

Given the lack of success of the "Rosie" set, the Music Committee changed course. However, they failed to act quickly. On June 3, 1986, they were still considering whether the contest ballad would be "Sonny Boy," or "I'd Love to Meet that Old Sweetheart of Mine," even though the latter song had never been rehearsed by the chorus.[95] In January 1987, a memo indicated that chapter members were having serious trouble learning the lyrics of songs.[96] By this time, the decreased performance quality was taking a toll on membership, coupled with anger from the membership over being overbilled by the competition hotel in Lake Placid. Regular attendance had declined to 30–32 members per meeting, but the chorus anticipated that 35–37 men would be present at the district competition. The disparity between these two data points can only indicate that the chorus was allowing onto the contest risers members who were not regularly attending the meetings.[97] The setting of annual goals appears to have fallen by the wayside, to be replaced by critiques of particular problems, such as the lack of a unit sound, the lack of section unity among the leads and a plea for members to learn their notes.[98] While the chorus improved at Division, they did not improve at Districts. The Chapter decided that the time had come for a major change.

After the District Contest in 1987, Ray Wixted submitted his letter of resignation. The Board had learned its lesson from the rather ugly dismissal of Tony Grosz. Ray Wixted was a beloved figure and a charter member of the chapter. His resignation was entirely of his own accord, though it may have been hinted to him that perhaps it was time for a change.[99] At the board meeting on November 5, 1987, his resignation was unanimously accepted. The board appointed John LaBosco as the acting director "until a new director is found," and nominated a search committee comprised of John LaBosco, Dick Zang, and Bill Manion to search for a new director.[100] The next month, the Board approved the creation of a Vice President of Music position and filled that position with John LaBosco, thereby upgrading the importance of music. At the same time, the Board proposed, and approved, giving Ray Wixted a gift of a lifetime membership in the society for his eleven years of directing the chorus at the cost of $750.[101]

Under Ray Wixted's direction, the chorus reached the zenith of its achievements. The chapter achieved its highest membership under him in late 1976. It achieved its highest division score, winning the division twice in 1980 and 1982, and it achieved its highest district placement by coming in fifth in the district twice, in 1977 and 1981. Yet under Wixted's direction, the chapter decline in musical standards in the mid-1980s led inexorably to a decline in membership. In a vicious cycle, that decline in membership further eroded the chorus's ability to present artfully sung music.

Wixted deserves neither all the credit for the Mad Hatter's successes nor all the blame for its failures. The successes of the chapter in his era were largely a result of the excitement and continued application of initiatives personally put in place by Tony Grosz, such as the Danbury Challenge Cup, and due to the fact that Wixted inherited a huge chorus of good singers who were just reaching their peak.

On the other hand, Wixted's failures to maintain vocal quality are also attributable to external factors. The demographics of Danbury were changing. The rise and fall of Union Carbide is a good example. That major manufacturer, which arrived in Danbury with such fanfare in the early 1980s, never recovered from the Bhopal disaster of 1984. A gas leak at a Union Carbide-owned pesticide plant in India resulted in the death of an estimated 14,000 people and in more than 730,000 cases of personal injury.[102] The disaster ruined the company's reputation and financial health, causing the jobs it had created in Danbury to evaporate.

In the meanwhile, the demographics of the chapter were changing. No longer could the chapter claim a membership of relatively young men,

2.10 (opposite) Sterling Edition

and obituary statements for founding and former members were becoming increasingly common. Wixted could not recreate the atmosphere that dominated under Grosz's leadership, when rehearsals featured not only good competition and quality singing, but also great entertainment and fun. Perhaps in part this was because of the divisions and bitterness that were left in the wake of Tony Grosz's dismissal. Whatever the reason, when Wixted and the Music Committee demanded strict qualifications, they faced a rebellion of the membership; but when they focused on retaining membership, they faced a decline in vocal quality that only exacerbated the membership issue. It was a Hobson's choice, and under the circumstances, Wixted did a truly remarkable job at the helm of the chorus.

Notes

1 Merkling, "Madhatters: 83 in four part harmony," 1.

2 Stebbins, *The Barbershop Singer*, 88.

3 "Census of Population and Housing," US Census Bureau, http://www.census.gov/prod/www/decennial.html.

4 Devlin and Janick, *Danbury's Third Century*, 267–270.

5 Merkling, "Madhatters: 83 in four part harmony," 1.

6 *Ibid.*

7 Bill Manion, personal interview, March 17, 2016.

8 Anton Grosz, personal interview, May 2, 2016.

9 Ray Waldron, "Danbury's Fantastic Membership Growth," *Nor'easter: The Voice of NED Barbershopper* XVII:2 (Feb. 1975):1.

10 Dick Zang, personal interview, February 16, 2016.

11 Minutes of Board of Directors, Danbury Chorus, January 4, June 7, and August 7, 1973.

12 Minutes of Board of Directors, Danbury Chorus, February 5, 1974.

13 Dick Zang, personal interview, May 3, 2016; Minutes of Board of Directors, Danbury Chorus, October 4, and December 6, 1973.

14 Minutes of Board of Directors, Danbury Chorus June 7, 1973.

15 Minutes of Board of Directors, Danbury Chorus Dec. 6, 1973.

16 "Chorus Plans Public Singing," *The News-Times* (Nov. 18, 1973).

17 NED "Official Scoring Summary: District Chorus Contest, 1974," Danbury Mad Hatter Scrapbook 1966–1980, Chorus Archive.

18 Minutes of Board of Directors, Danbury Chorus, February 5, 1974.

19 Waldron, "Danbury's Fantastic Membership Growth," 7.

20 "Quartet Corner," *The Hatter Chatter* (October 1975), 1.

21 *Ibid.*

22 Dick Zang, personal interview, May 2, 2016; Minutes of Board of Directors, Danbury Chorus, November 7, 1974.

23 Anton Grosz, personal interview, May 2, 2016.

24 Dick Zang, personal interview, February 16, 2016.

25 This statement requires two caveats: The Reunion Quartet, which won Districts in 1989, included one member from Danbury. Two quartets with Danbury members have competed at international: the Pretenders in 1967 and the Brotherhood (Anton Grosz was still officially a Danbury member at the time), in 1976.

26 NED "Official Scoring Summary: District Chorus Contest, Montreal, Oct 25, 1975," Danbury Mad Hatter Scrapbook 1966–1980, Chorus Archive.

27 "While Having a Good Time, Local Barbershop Singers Promote Peace, Tranquility," *The Monroe Courier* (June 11, 1975), 1.

28 Letter from Gerry Otton to Anton Grosz, July 1975, 1973–1980 documents binder, Chorus Archive.

29 It is unclear what the status of the 1971 qualification rules written by then Director Bill Manion and the music committee were at this point in 1975.

30 Memo from the Music Director to the Music Committee and the Board of Directors, July 29, 1975. 1973–1980 documents binder, Chorus Archive.

31 Dick Zang, personal interview, May 2, 2016.

32 Minutes of Board of Directors, October 2, 1975.

33 Minutes of Board of Directors, May 13, 1976.

34 Bob Connolley, personal interview, April 20, 2016.

35 Minutes of Board of Directors, Danbury Chorus, June 3, 1976.

36 Minutes of Board of Directors, Danbury Chorus, Nov 5,1987.

37 Dick Zang, personal interview, February 16, 2016.

38 Ray Waldron, "Danbury's Fantastic Membership Growth," 1.

39 Bob Connolley, personal interview, April 20, 2016.

40 *Ibid.*

41 Jack Cramer, email to author, August 13, 2016.

42 Bob Stewart, email to author, August 16, 2016.

43 Jack Cramer, emails to author, August 13 and August 16, 2016.

44 *Ibid.*

45 Anton Grosz, personal interview, May 2, 2016.

46 Anton Grosz, *a Dying Friend: Helping Those You Love Make a Conscious Transition* (Wheaton, IL: Thosophical Publishing House, 1989), ix-9.

47 Letter from the Music Staff to Chorus Members, January 1, 1977, Danbury Scrapbook 1966–1980, Chorus Archive.

48 "Goals for Music Staff and Chorus (December 1976). 1973–1980 documents binder, Chorus Archive.

49 *Ibid.*

50 Letter from the Music Staff to Chorus Members, January 1, 1977, Danbury Scrapbook 1966–1980, Chorus Archive.

51 Letter from Music Staff to Members of Danbury Chorus, January 1, 1977.

52 Ray Wixted, notes on 1977 division contest, Danbury Scrapbook 1966–1980, Chorus Archive.

53 "Man Alive! We're Number 5!" *Hatter Chatter* (Oct-Nov 1977):1.

54 Dick Zang, personal interview, February 16, 2016; Bill Manion, personal interview, March 17, 2016.

55 "Membership Classification: Fourth Quarter, 1977." 1973–1980 documents binder, Chorus Archive.

56 "Francis Golden," *Artists in Stock: Pierce Galleries Ltd.* Accessed October 21, 2016. http://www.piercegalleries.com/artists/iart_golden.html; Jack Cramer, Email to Author, August 15, 2016.

57 Jack Cramer, Email to Author, August 16, 2016.

58 "Music Keys Wixted," *Danbury News-Times* (November 27, 1977), 1; "Raymond Wixted: Obituary," *The News-Times* (April 11, 2012).

59 "My Home Town," 1977 Annual Show Program, Danbury Scrapbook 1966–1980, Chorus Archive.

60 Keith McIntyre (as secretary for the Ad Hoc Committee), "Meeting on Why New Membership is Hard to Come By," (July 18, 1978), 1973–1980 documents binder, Chorus Archive.

61 Minutes of Board of Directors, Danbury Chorus, Sept 7, 1978.

62 "New York Show," (Sept 29, 1978), 1973–1980 documents binder, Chorus Archive.

63 Minutes of Board of Directors, Danbury Chorus, March 1, 1979.

64 "Girls, Girls, Girls!" 1979 Annual Show Program, Danbury Mad Hatter Scrapbook 1966–1980, Chorus Archive.

65 Minutes of Board of Directors, Danbury Chorus, Jan 10, 1980.

66 *Ibid.*

67 *Ibid.*

68 "Music Committee," (November 4, 1980), 1973–1980 documents binder, Chorus Archive.

69 Memo from Bill Manion (Music Comm. Chairman) to the Board of Directors (Jan 13, 1981), 1981–1984 documents binder, Chorus Archive.

70 Dick Zang, "The Way We Were," *Hatter Chatter* 21:7 (August 2014):4.

71 Harmony Earns Honors for Madhatters," *The News-Times (*March 11, 1982):15.

72 Jack Cramer, "1982 Goals," 1981–1984 Documents binder, Chorus Archive.

73 "Craft Program," (July 1982), 1981–1984 Documents binder, Chorus Archive.

74 Minutes of the Music Committee Meeting, August 10, 1982, 1981–1984 Documents binder, Chorus Archive.

75 1982 Protection Achievement Scores, 1981–1984 Documents binder, Chorus Archive.

76 Jack Cramer, "President's Message," (December 1982), 1981–1984 Documents binder, Chorus Archive.

77 Memo from Jack Cramer to Ray Wixted and Bill Manion (March 15, 1983), 1981–1984 Documents binder, Chorus Archive.

78 Memo from Jack Cramer to Bill Manion (July 12, 1983), 1981–1984 Documents binder, Chorus Archive.

79 Memo from Bill Manion to Jack Cramer, (August 9, 1983), 1981–1984 Documents binder, Chorus Archive.

80 Official scoring summary, District Quartet Contest, Semi-Final Round, Providence, RI, October 21, 1983, 1983–1985 Documents binder, Chorus Archive.

81 "Summer Happenings," *Hatter Chatter* (Sept 1983):4–5.

82 Ray Wixted, "Notes on Critique of Mad Hatter's October 22, 1983 Providence, Rhode Island, district competition," 1981–1984 Documents binder, Chorus Archive.

83 Minutes of the Board of Directors, held at the Elks Club, December 15, 1983.

84 "Danbury Chapter: 1984 Goals," 1981–1984 Documents binder, Chorus Archive.

85 "Rapid Improvement in Singing Excellence (RISE): A New Program for Chorus Improvement," 1981–1984 Documents binder, Chorus Archive.

86 1984 Music Committee Budget, 1981–1984 Documents binder, Chorus Archive.

87 Minutes of the Music Committee Meeting, March 19, 1984, 1981–1984 Documents binder, Chorus Archive.

88 "Subject: Search for New Meeting Facilities," 1985–1987 Documents binder, Chorus Archive.

89 1985 Annual Show Report, in 1985–1987 Documents binder, Chorus Archive.

90 Official scoring summary, NED Division III Chorus Contest, East Hartford, Conn., May 4, 1985. 1985–1987 Documents binder, Chorus Archive.

91 *Ibid.*

92 Minutes of Board of Directors, Danbury Chorus, Nov 7, 1985.

93 Ray Wixted, "Directorially Speaking," *Hatter Chatter* (Feb. 1986), 1.

94 Minutes of the Music Committee, February 11, 1986, 1985–1987 Documents binder, Chorus Archive.

95 Minutes of the Music Committee, June 3, 1986, 1985–1987 Documents binder, Chorus Archive.

96 "Calendar for January, February, and March 1987," 1985–1987 Documents binder, Chorus Archive.

97 Minutes of Board of Directors, Danbury Chorus, Feb 5, 1987.

98 Ray Wixted, "Madhatter Chorus: Six Month Program," 1985–1987 Documents binder, Chorus Archive.

99 Bill Manion, personal interview, March 17, 2016.

100 Minutes of Board of Directors, Danbury Chapter, Nov 5, 1987.

101 Minutes of Board of Directors, Danbury Chapter, Feb 5, 1987.

102 Ingrid Eckerman, *The Bhopal Saga: Causes and Consequences of the World's Largest Industrial Disaster* (Hyderabad, India: Universities Press, 2005).

3 "Maintaining the Tonal Center"
Struggling for Existence in a Changing World, 1987–2002

As the Danbury chapter struggled in the late 1980s, they were certainly not alone in their troubles. The peak year of membership in the Danbury chapter corresponds perfectly with the peak year of membership in the Society as a whole: 1976. Interest in the Danbury Chapter waned in direct proportion with interest in barbershop in general. In the words of Richard Mook, "in the 1980s the Society confronted a decline and demographic shift in its membership: barbershoppers were aging, and fewer young singers were joining." Youth outreach efforts from the society "produced limited results," and an "urgency persist[ed] concerning the recruitment of new, especially younger, members." Equally serious was a concern "about a lack of racial and ethnic diversity," bringing about generally unsuccessful efforts to "seek diversity as a response to the challenges of aging and declining membership."[1]

In fact, the problem was not even as specific to barbershop as that explanation makes it seem. From card playing to churchgoing to volunteering to voting, since the 1970s Americans have consistently rejected group-oriented social activities that animated the lives of people of previous generations. The explanations for this larger trend are hard to pinpoint, but they range from the increasing need of breadwinners to work two or three jobs to make ends meet, to the inordinate amount of time spent on commuting due to urban sprawl, to the devotion of Americans to solitary activities based on technology platforms such as video games and other mass media.² In an economic system in which more and more families must have two income earners to survive, in which people have to drive long distances through heavy traffic to get from home to work, how could people find the time for barbershop?

These problems, which have been endemic in American society since the 1980s, hit the Danbury area with even more force. The kind of technology and manufacturing jobs that spurred the growth of cities like Danbury were in serious decline and with them a middle class containing men with free leisure time on their hands. In the 1990s, Danbury's new jobs were increasingly to be found only in the service sector. These jobs, such as those created when more than 200 stores opened in the new Danbury Fair Mall in the fall of 1986, generally paid much lower wages, forcing workers to work more hours to make ends meet, and leaving much less time for "hobbies" such as barbershop.³

Moreover, the population of western Connecticut was becoming considerably less white. Between 2000 and 2006, the number of Connecticut residents born in India jumped 94 percent; the number born in Brazil jumped 82 percent, and the number born in Ecuador jumped 74 percent. Meanwhile, the number born in Italy declined 13 percent.⁴ By 2006, Danbury had a larger foreign-born population than any city in Connecticut, at 34 percent.⁵

Joseph DaSilva, an enterprising former baker from the Azores, an archipelago in the mid-Atlantic that is also an autonomous region of Portugal, began buying property in Danbury's downtown area in the late 1960s. He subdivided those properties to form affordable housing. In the 1970s, from his office in the former building of the Danbury News-Times on Main Street, DaSilva managed a rental empire. By the time of his death in 1983, he owned more than 100 properties, mostly on Main Street and Liberty Street.⁶ He provided housing opportunities for Danbury's burgeoning Portuguese and Brazilian population. By 2002, there were more than 10,000 Portuguese-speaking Brazilians in Danbury and the surrounding towns. By that year, Danbury also boasted many more people from Cambodia, the Dominican Republic, and Ecuador. The city also had the second largest population of people from India in the state.[7]

How were the Danbury Mad Hatters to attract a population of men who were working multiple jobs in the service sector, or living in two income families, with little disposable income and even less available time, who had grown up listening to salsa or *bossa nova* or Cambodian poprock, to come to a rehearsal at an aging building of an increasingly irrelevant fraternal order and sing music that was popular among the white middle class at the turn of the twentieth century? Recruitment efforts encountered insurmountable demographic headwinds.

And so, the Mad Hatter Chorus struggled mightily in the late 1980s and through the 1990s, not only because of its own weaknesses, but also because of the weight of social and cultural changes to which it could not adjust. By January 1988, the Vice President for Membership of the Chorus reported that although the number of official members was still a very healthy sixty-five, the number attending the Tuesday night meetings in January was only twenty.[8] In June of 1988, member Dan Duda wrote to the Music Committee to complain that the song repertoire, which consisted of over forty songs in early 1987, was rapidly deteriorating. While officially the repertoire had not declined, in practice much of it was no longer being performed. The chapter was increasingly singing "polecats," a set of simple, short songs known universally by Barbershoppers. The Music Committee was trying to address that by introducing the new song "Are You From Dixie?" Duda approved of this, but considered it to be too small a gesture.[9]

The problem could not necessarily be laid at the feet of the Mad Hatters' director. John LaBosco of New Milford was a long-time baritone in the chorus and a talented musician who was a music teacher himself.[10] LaBosco went on to become a successful director of the Palmetto Statesman of the Spartanburg, North Carolina chapter, well into the 2010s.[11] Yet he appears to have been very deferential to the Board and to the music team, led by Andre Lesperance, and appears to not have been able to assert himself as a major factor in improving attendance or singing.

Based on the comments of Duda and others, in May 1988, the chapter set the following short term goals: to increase membership by fifteen percent from the end of 1987, to improve morale by varying the program at the chapter meetings and announcing them in advance, by having more sing-outs, and by having more fun. Additionally, the chorus set out to create, and adhere to, "vocal standards," and to improve communications both internally and with inactive and past members. A note at the bottom indicated that the result of a discussion of finally creating a formal wives' auxiliary was of interest but was not to be included as a goal.[12] While these were admirable goals, it is notable how little the goals had changed since 1985, and the Board did not establish how those goals were to be achieved, which was important considering that they had failed to achieve similar goals in the recent past.

The Mad Hatters found that making headway on the membership goal was difficult. By August 1988, membership had dropped to fifty-five, though actual attendance was stable at twenty. By December, some progress had been made, with average attendance in November at the supplemental rehearsals for the annual show up to thirty-seven. Some improvement in morale had also been made by allocating chapter funds for "wives' appreciation nights," in which the chapter would pay for a dinner for families and the chorus would entertain members' wives. Moreover, the Chapter show seems to have generated excitement and caused some inactive members to return. The chorus turned a heady profit of $3,500 on the 1988 show.[13]

In 1989, Bob Bartley took over as president. He aimed to focus on establishing clear procedures. He proclaimed at a board meeting that the chapter would "not wing it as we have in the past; we will have procedures to follow." Concomitant with this focus on procedure, Bartley announced that the chapter goals for 1989 would emphasize discipline and professionalism. The goals were: for the chorus to give the director its undivided attention, and for the chorus to act professionally on stage.[14] Though these seem like worthy items to communicate to the members, to articulate them as goals seems in hindsight to be incredibly myopic. It seems doubtful that an inactive member, upon learning that the chorus was going to set a goal to pay more attention to the director, would be motivated to activate his membership.

There was considerable resistance to Bob Bartley's leadership almost from the start. At the end of January 1989, immediate past president Bob Stanczak penned a letter to Bartley explaining his decision to resign as editor of the *Hatter Chatter*. Stanczak was upset because, contrary to "the custom of this chapter," he was not recognized or thanked by Bartley for his service as the previous Chapter President at the installation dinner, which Stanczak took as "a personal affront." However, he made clear that the letter was not "as self-serving" as it might seem, because this kind of affront was "symptomatic of a growing problem."[15]

That problem with Bartley's leadership was one that was not confined to Stanczak, but has been reported by several members recalling that time. The major objection of the Mad Hatters to Bartley's leadership style was based on the lack of deference he showed to Joe Talarico, a founding member who had been the pillar of the chapter from its inception. He was not the strongest singer, but more than any other individual member, he is remembered for being responsible for the growth of the chorus and its reputation as the most fun-loving chorus in the district. Talarico's backyard sing-outs would bring people from blocks around to taste his signature corn and sausage and listen to the quartets. His antics as one of the leads in the VLQ "Octet" in the 1970s produced more than one memorable act in annual shows.[16] This VLQ memorably featured Ed Van Derzee and Len Carlson, who were both well over six feet tall. They would sandwich the 5-foot-4-inch Talarico and use a mechanism in their Stetson hats to drench him with water.[17]

In 1988, Talarico had become ill with cancer and was forced to leave the chapter. This motivated old-timers in the Mad Hatters to visit him. Bill

Manion, for example, fondly remembers going to Talarico's house to play —and lose—at cards to him. In preparation for the installation dinner in 1989, Stanczak and other chorus members had prepared a testimonial tribute to Talarico, and approached Bartley to ask for chapter funds to pay for a gift for this valuable, ill, and departing founding member. According to the letter, Bartley replied that he "didn't think it was proper to use chapter funds for such things because we would be setting a precedent." This was an insensitive and inconsistent response, considering that such parting gifts had regularly been given to departing Presidents, Show Chairmen, and Directors as a matter of course. In fact, less than two years earlier, the chorus had given Ray Wixted a lifetime membership worth $750.[18] Regardless of the motivations involved, Bartley's decision caused great resentment and consternation among many of the longest-tenured members of the chapter.

Upon receiving Stanczak's letter, Bartley did not apologize. His solution to the problem, which was to draw up a long and complicated manual detailing the procedure by which the President was to thank the Past President, clearly showed that he did not comprehend the emotional issues involved.[19] This wound was only made deeper in the spring of 1989 when Talarico passed away, and his wife Rita received an official letter of condolence from the society on the occasion of the death of her husband "James" Talarico.[20]

In the spring of 1989, even the Board meetings became chaotic and contentious. At the end of the minutes of the March 1989 meeting, Secretary Daniel Duda commented: "How can the Board expect discipline from the chorus when the Board itself lacks discipline? Listen to my tape. Our board meeting sounds like the Morton Downey, Jr. Show. It is difficult taking minutes when six people are talking at the same time."[21] The meeting on May 11, 1989 was so heated that the arguments lasted for four hours and thirty-five minutes.[22]

There was an additional reason for the rancor. Early in 1989, John LaBosco had left abruptly, leading to a chorus director search. By April

1989, Mike Cohen was emerging as a favorite to become the new director. Though the application of Mike Cohen, who was not yet a member of the Mad Hatters, was rushed to approval in a special board meeting on May 2, 1989, he was not appointed director at the regular May meeting as expected. Rather, after a heated discussion of more than twenty minutes, the board chose to take no action.[23] At the June 1989 meeting, a compromise position was reached. George Schwerdt and Mike Cohen would be co-directors, with Don Sutherland as assistant director.[24] In the meantime, a very controversial movement arose on the board to try to reject the renewal applications of inactive members, which, if approved, would have decimated chapter quartets.[25]

Slowly, disagreements on the Board began to have an effect on the rest of the membership. Because of the chaos in the director's position, new programs and music were not ready, and a guest night had to be cancelled. In the meantime, non-participating members reported to the board that they were "dissatisfied because they weren't having any fun."[26] Regular attendance at events began to fall below twenty on a consistent basis.[27]

As the calendar turned to 1990, and Bob Bartley continued his tenure as president for another year, things began to fall apart. The chapter had lost more than $4,000 in revenue between 1988 and 1989, necessitating an internal audit of its books.[28] Only sixteen members had shown up to perform in Danbury's First Night Celebrations, which was becoming a staple performance of the chapter and would be for the next twenty-five years.[29] By the February meeting, long-time member and secretary Daniel Duda had become so frustrated that he began recording irrelevant and digressive *ad hominem* discussions at meetings, such as one about the program book (which Program Vice President Rocco Bonanducci called "the worst program I've ever seen in my life"), verbatim into the minutes.[30]

The chorus was also plagued by turnover at the director position. Mike Cohen left the chapter abruptly early in 1990, and the directorship then devolved to George Schwerdt, with Don Sutherland continuing as the Assistant Director.[31] As a result, the music team was behind on its planning. Despite the Music Team's being in the capable hands of Music Vice President Dick Zang, no show music had been discussed despite a resolution from the board to agree on show music by the beginning of the year. The contest music, "How 'Ya Gonna Keep 'Em Down on the Farm?" and "When You and I Were Young, Maggie," had been decided on, but four months after these songs had been chosen, no preparation had been made for contest choreography.[32]

The March 1990 meeting minutes are sufficient to demonstrate a Danbury chapter in dysfunction and disarray. They feature a Music Committee report from Dick Zang indicating that he believed that there would not be a sufficient number of members on stage to have a good performance at the division contest and that many members did not know the words and music to the two songs they expected to perform, despite their both being old songs. Then a twenty-minute discussion ensued in which members pointed out that the Board had resolved in their previous meeting to approach George Schwerdt about becoming the new director, but no one had actually approached him. Meanwhile, George Schwerdt had read the minutes and was wondering why no one had actually asked him to be director.[33] To add to the confusion, by June, Cohen actually reversed himself and retook the helm as director, though he would not stay long.

In the midst of the chaos into which the chorus was descending, one bright spot that remained was the strength of the chapter quartets. The Connecticut Wailers, featuring Bob Leety on tenor, Ray Wixted on lead, John LaBosco on baritone, and Dick Zang on bass, was a popular competition quartet in the late 1980s. The Right Blend, which was a kind of successor to the Wailers, was a very successful variety and comedy quartet featuring George Schwerdt on tenor, Ray Wixted on lead, Carl Binder on baritone, and Bob Connolley on bass. In the midst of the total disintegration of the chorus, the Right Blend was successful in competition. At the Division Three quartet contest in Milford, Connecticut, in 1991,

3.1 (opposite) The Connecticut Wailers

they not only captured the novice championship, but also won the entire division, with very high scores in interpretation. Their total score at that contest was a 430, and in that year, the lowest score at the international competition was a 443.[34]

But this modicum of success was not enough to change the direction of the chorus. Frustrated with the quality of singing and the acrimony of the board, the Membership Vice President Bob Torielli and the Program

3.2 *The Right Blend*

Vice President Rocco Bonanducci abruptly resigned on August 16, 1990.[35] At a special board meeting held on August 27, it was "unanimously decided to cancel" the annual show "due to the lack of turn out at weekly meetings and the short time in which to get ready by the scheduled October 13 show date."[36] In November 1990, the upcoming installation dinner was also cancelled.[37] At the end of Bob Bartley's term in 1990, three board members had left. These included long-time secretary Dan Duda, who had resigned as a member of the chapter in July, saying that he "had another hobby" that he found more enjoyable "and plan[ned] to devote more time to it." He did, however, stay on as secretary until the end of the year.

Starting in 1991, the records of the Mad Hatters also descend into chaos and disorganization. Meeting minutes only begin to appear again

3.3 *(opposite) The Mad Hatters at the Division Contest, Norwich, CT, April 1990*

in 1994. But the contest experience does tell a clear story. In 1992, Don Sutherland had replaced George Schwerdt as director. At the division contest in April of that year, the Mad Hatters had fifteen men on the risers. In 1993, under the co-direction of Don Sutherland and Bill Manion, the Mad Hatters improved somewhat in their participation, with eighteen men on the risers. In 1994, under Bill Manion, the chorus fielded twenty for the division contest. Active membership was stabilizing at around twenty, but in none of these years did the Mad Hatters make it to the district competition.

In 1994, under the tenure of competent and conscientious secretary Bill Gleissner, records for the chorus begin to reappear. At that point, the Mad Hatters had an Acting President, Wes Pollitt, who was also the membership VP. One problem of the chorus at the time was that no one was recording or distributing learning tapes. This had been an issue since the late 1980s.[38] Meanwhile, the facilities at the Elks Club continued to deteriorate. Already by the early 1990s, the Elks were no longer serving food in the Rathskeller, and the chorus was prevented from putting risers on the stage because of fire code issues. Now the chorus was being removed from the main dining room during various chapter meetings at the whim of the Elks.[39]

Despite Pollitt's efforts, membership continued to deteriorate. His personal notes from the end of 1994 tell the story well. They list current losses of members to that date and the reasons for the loss. From the fall of 1993 to the fall of 1994, the chorus lost ten members, many of whom had been in it for decades. Dick Zang left in September 1993 because there were "no quartet opportunities." Former President Gerry Otten left because "the learning process was too slow." John Noonan, John Logan, and George King "lost interest." Jim Hopper only had time for quartetting. Don Fox and Bob Bartley said there were no quartetting opportunities and rehearsals were no fun. Dave Cortez had family obligations. Denis Couture was working the night shift as a custodian.[40] Together, the combination of extrinsic and interpersonal factors was causing the remaining long-standing members to leave.

Dick Zang remembers precisely how bad things were. Sometime during the tenure of Don Sutherland as director, he got a call. Don wanted him to learn the baritone part for contest. The reason this was necessary was that there were currently zero baritones able to go to contest; indeed, there were almost no active baritones in the chapter. Dick Zang took him up on this request, but the story is emblematic of the kinds of problems that caused him to leave.[41] Only a little more than a decade removed from the pinnacle of its success, the Danbury chapter was suddenly on the verge of becoming extinct.

There were attempts by the board to address these issues. By August 1994, the board was implementing learning tapes, section rehearsals, and quartet games at chapter meetings as a high priority means to try to increase quality singing, quartetting, and fun.[42] In 1995, under the leadership of Music Director Bill Manion and President Ed Harvey, the chorus reinstituted the "Show Glow," in which barbershopping was combined with dinner and other entertainment. Wes Pollitt put a big effort into guest nights, sending out hundreds of invitations. Reading the minutes of those years, however, there is a feeling that the members were bailing water on the Titanic. The 1995 Guest Night "was not a huge success" despite the efforts involved.[43] The membership would rise into the low forties, then fall back down, despite the considerable effort being undertaken; moreover, at all times, the actual attendance at meetings was much, much lower.

In 1996, an extraordinary effort to revive flagging membership was made by handing out to members a list of 116 prospects for each member to call. The Board even contemplated paying outright for the memberships of current members who were letting their memberships expire, though that motion eventually failed.[44] The Board had by this time brought Ray Wixted back for a third stint as director, and he took a much more active role, offering critiques of the length and format of the Show Glow.[45]

In 1998, the Mad Hatter Chorus, still under the direction of Ray Wixted, performed "I Want a Girl" and "I'm Looking Over a Four Leaf Clover," at the Division Contest in Highland, New York. They came in seventh, next to last, only beating out New London's Sea Notes, but they were able to get a bid to districts, where they placed twentieth—dead last. The judges' comments indicate individual voices sticking out, tuning problems, exposure of vibrato, clipping the ends of words, and making major keys minor. The chorus scored "slightly under a middle C" in the singing category. The conclusion gleaned from the summary was "we are ok singers with unexploited potential. We need improvement on basic vocal production and singing support."[46] At the August 1998 meeting, Ray Wixted "asked the board to accept his resignation as director, citing personal frustration in the progress of the chorus." His resignation was "accepted with regret."[47]

At the 1999 Division contest, the Mad Hatters fielded twenty-five members on the risers and sang "Heart of My Heart" and "Listen to that Dixie Band" complete with instruments. They placed eighth in a field with twelve competitors. Their score did not improve. The chorus was aware of the singing problems. A summary of the Music Committee report in May 1998 indicated that "we are behind on our qualifications for new songs, our stage performance sucks, we need to sing like we do in rehearsal, we are not listening to each other, therefore we are not matching sound or vowels."[48] In 2000, the chorus, co-directed by Don Sutherland and Bill Manion, placed dead last in the division contest in Manchester, Connecticut, singing "Carolina in the Morning," and "Oh, You Beautiful Doll."

Despite the apparently awful singing quality, the late 1990s brought signs of improvement in the overall health of the chapter. This was a chorus that, in the words of President Bob Bradley and Secretary (and brother) John Bradley, frequently "sucked" (the latter being a word that appears shockingly frequently in the Board meeting minutes of the late 1990s). Bob Bradley, a former campaign coordinator who currently runs a real estate agency in Carmel, New York, was a relatively new member of the Mad Hatters, but he had the low-key attitude and the work ethic to succeed as President.[49] The Mad Hatters were now somewhat jovial about their "suck level," and they were willing to raise it. More importantly, Bob Bradley and his colleagues brought back the sense of camaraderie and fun that had always been the hallmark of the chorus before the conflicts of the early 1990s.

Bob Bradley managed to slowly increase morale despite the fact that during the late 1990s and early 2000s the board, with key members including Steve Horhota, Bob Bartley, John Bradley, Dick Walter, Don Smith, and Tom McCarthy, continued to have contentious and long chapter meetings and considerable disputes over the rules and finances of the still-cash-strapped chorus. Nevertheless, things began to come together. After Wixted's (second) resignation, Bill Manion and Don Sutherland, who had teamed up to handle music for the chorus as early as the late 1960s, led the music side of the chorus once again. They certainly had the experience to work with one another. They were joined by the capable and talented tenor Steve Horhota.

For these reasons, despite the poor quality of singing from the group in this period, the chapter was maintaining and even growing membership. In 1998, the chorus gained twelve new members and achieved a 96%

membership retention rate in 1998. A membership survey in April 1999 revealed that "overall, chapter members seem to be pleased with how things are progressing for the chapter."[50]

However, they were still stuck in a musical rut. Therefore, the Mad Hatters decided to throw all their energy into a youth movement. In October 2002, the chorus, under the urging of Bill Manion and others, was developing relationships with local high schools and with Western Connecticut State University. They were able to get a young music student named Joel Knecht to join them. Joel was the fresh face the Mad Hatters needed at the time, and he wanted experience directing a chorus. The Mad Hatters' youth movement would follow.

Notes

1 Richard Mook, "Barbershop," in John Shepherd, David Horn (eds.), *Popular Music of the World Volume 8* (London: A and C Black, 2008).

2 For a thorough analysis of these trends, see Robert D. Putnam, *Bowling Alone: The Collapse and Revival of American Community* (New York: Simon and Schuster, 2001).

3 Edward C. Sembor, *An Introduction to Connecticut State and Local Government* (Lanham, MD: University Press of America, 2003), 115; Devlin and Janick, Danbury's Third Century, 288–289.

4 Rafael Mejia and Priscilla Canny, Ph.D. *Immigration in Connecticut: A Growing Opportunity* (New Haven: CT Kids Link, 2007), 5.

5 *Ibid.*, 3.

6 Devlin and Janick, *Danbury's Third Century*, 290.

7 Mike Swift, "A Worldly Place," *Hartford Courant* (Jan 13, 2002).

8 Minutes of Board of Directors, Danbury Chapter, Feb 11, 1988.

9 Dan Duda, "Where Have My Old Songs Gone?" 1988–1990 Documents binder.

10 Dick Zang, personal interview, May 5, 2016.

11 "The Palmetto Statesmen," Retrieved May 5, 2016. http://www.carolinasdistrict.org/wpcontent/uploads/2015/10/2011charterchapters.pdf.

12 Attachment to Agenda for the Board Meeting, May 5, 1988, 1988–1990 Documents binder, Danbury Chapter, Chorus Archive.

13 Minutes of Board of Directors, Danbury Chapter, Jan 5, 1989.

14 Minutes of Board of Directors, Danbury Chapter, Feb 2, 1989.

15 Letter from Immediate Past President Bob Stanczak to President Bob Bartley, January 24, 1989. 1988–1990 Documents binder, Chorus Archive.

16 Dick Zang, personal interview, February 16, 2016; Bill Manion, personal interview, March 17, 2016; Bob Connolley, personal interview, April 20, 2016.

17 Bill Manion, "A Thank You from Bill Manion," *Hatter Chatter* 23:5 (August 2016):3.

18 Dick Zang, personal interview, February 16, 2016.

19 Minutes of Board of Directors, Danbury Chapter, Feb 2, 1989.

20 Minutes of Board of Directors, Danbury Chapter, May 11, 1989.

21 Minutes of Board of Directors, Danbury Chapter, March 9, 1989.

22 Minutes of Board of Directors, Danbury Chapter, May 11, 1989.

23 *Ibid.*

24 Minutes of Board of Directors, Danbury Chapter, June 8, 1989.

25 Letter from Daniel Duda to the Board of Directors, June 1989. 1988–1990 Documents binder, Chorus Archive.

26 Minutes of Board of Directors, Danbury Chapter, Aug 24, 1989.

27 Minutes of Board of Directors, Danbury Chapter, Sept 7, 1989.

28 Minutes of Board of Directors, Danbury Chapter, Jan 11, 1990.

29 *Ibid.*

30 Minutes of Board of Directors, Danbury Chapter, Feb 8, 1990.

31 *Ibid.*

32 *Ibid.*

33 Minutes of Board of Directors, Danbury Chapter, Mar 15, 1990.

34 "Official Scoring Summary, Division Three Quartet Contest," the information on the international contest provided by Bob Connolley's notations on the sheet.

35 Minutes of Board of Directors, Danbury Chapter, Aug 16, 1990.

36 Minutes of Board of Directors, Special Meeting, Aug 27, 1990.

37 Minutes of Board of Directors, Danbury Chapter, Nov 8, 1990.

38 Minutes of Board of Directors, Danbury Chapter, June 2. 1994.

39 *Ibid*.

40 Wes Pollitt, "Membership Notes," 1994–1997 Documents binder, Chorus Archive.

41 Dick Zang, personal communication, May 5, 2016.

42 Minutes of Board of Directors, Danbury Chapter, Aug 2, 1994.

43 Minutes of Board of Directors, Danbury Chapter, June 8, 1995.

44 Minutes of Board of Directors, Danbury Chapter, July, 15, 1996.

45 Ray Wixted, "Show Glow Survey," (1996), 1994–1997 Documents binder, Chorus Archive.

46 "Summary of Judges' Critique, 1998 District Competition, Saratoga Springs, NY. 1998–2007 files, Chorus Archive.

47 Minutes of Board of Directors, Danbury Chapter, Aug 6, 1998.

48 Minutes of Board of Directors, Danbury Chapter, May 14, 1998.

49 "Robert Bradley: Immediate Past President." The Mad Hatter Chorus. Retrieved May 6, 2016. http://madhatterchorus.org/node/52.

50 Minutes of Board of Directors, Danbury Chapter, April 8, 1999.

4 "The Danbury Sound"
The Era of the Young Directors, 2002–2016

By 2002, the chorus was back on solid footing. Its membership, which famously had shrunk to twelve active members in the worst days of the 1990s, had stabilized, with membership consistently in the low thirties—where it remains today. The chapter was not growing exponentially, but it was not under any existential threat. Camaraderie and good administration were also present, and the attitude of the chorus improved steadily under the leadership of Bob Bradley, who had taken over as President in 1997 and would remain President until 2009.

However, the Mad Hatters stagnated from a singing and performance point of view. Bill Manion was now well into his third stint at directing the chorus, and he and the board were interested in bringing someone in who could offer fresh ideas. The chorus had made a conscious decision to try to focus on that goal by collaborating with young people. The Mad Hatters regularly invited Danbury High School's Madrigal Singers to perform on their annual show.[1] In May of 2002, the Mad Hatters attempted to use their connections with Danbury High to entice Patty Jimenez, the choral music teacher at Danbury High School, to become the director of the Mad Hatters.[2] This effort was apparently not successful.

Early in the fall of 2002, however, the Mad Hatters had a visitor from down the hill at Danbury's Western Connecticut State University. Joel Knecht was a music student at WCSU who already had "many years of barbershop experience and a college background in music and music theory." His experience included having formed a college barbershop quartet at WCSU. In approving his application for membership, the Board noted that he would be a "solid addition to the chorus."[3] But Music Director Bill Manion also saw this as an opportunity to infuse the chapter with the energy and new ideas of youth. At the November board meeting, Manion indicated that he would like "Joel to direct the chorus" for the division contest in the spring, and that the chapter should send him to the Society's Director's College in the summer of 2003.[4]

In the fall of 2002, with the blessing of Bill Manion and Don Sutherland, Knecht put together a detailed plan for the musical direction of the chorus for 2003. These included more structured rehearsals, a new procedure for learning songs through the section leaders, and an attempt to create more informal quartetting in the chapter. Based on this work, at their meeting on January 5, 2003, the Music Committee recommended to the board that Joel Knecht be formally made the Director of the Chorus, and that Bill Manion and Don Sutherland act as Assistant Directors as needed. At that meeting, Manion urged "every member to help Joel kick off his tenure in a very positive way. He has put a lot of thought into the Directorship and I, for one, believe his ideas are very sound."[5]

When Joel Knecht had joined the chorus, he had brought along a fellow singer, Joseph (Joe) Hudson. Originally from Stratford, Connecticut, Hudson was a music education major with extensive background in instrumental music (a trumpeter) and in musical theater. When he auditioned for a jazz combo at WCSU, someone overheard him say that he could sight-read music, and he was recruited for the college's barbershop quartet, for which Joel Knecht was singing bass. In 2002, Knecht drove Hudson to a Mad Hatters chapter meeting, and he filled out an application.[6]

Hudson became a member of the chorus in January 2003 and became an assistant director following the 2003 annual show. In the fall of 2003, he was responsible for leading warm-ups and craft work before

Knecht took over the main rehearsal.[7] Knecht also found new ways of encouraging the formation of quartets. He devised a scheme in which the chapter would select an official "chapter novice quartet" in the fall, and that the quartet would be asked to remain active for one year, compete in the division contest, and perform on the annual show. The next year, a new quartet would be selected.[8]

Though his novice quartet plan would never be implemented, Knecht's presence had an impact on quartetting and on the chorus. For many years, the only significant active quartet in the chapter had been Real Chemistry. Organized around 1998 and still active until 2016, this quartet originally featured Steve Horhota on tenor, Bob Bradley on lead, Art Roberts on baritone, and Dick Walter on bass. Around 2000, Art Roberts was replaced on baritone by John Bradley; around 2008, when Horhota moved away from the area, he was replaced by August "Augie" D'Aureli; D'Aureli was in turn replaced by Richard Schoonmaker in 2014. Real Chemistry made strides and even began competing. Shortly after Knecht placed an emphasis on quartetting, other new quartets began to emerge. In 2004, the Hattertones, originally featuring Joe Hudson on tenor, Dan Griffin on lead, Chuck Kreiger on baritone, and Ron Keith on bass, was formed. Both competed at the Division competition in West Hartford that year, placing at the bottom, as could be expected for newly competing quartets.

Under Knecht's leadership, the chorus began to perform better. Singing "I'll Be Seeing You" and "Oh, You Beautiful Doll" at the Yankee Division Contest in Saratoga Springs in April 2003, the chorus came in last, scoring a 53.4 with nineteen men on the risers. Their raw score, however, went up considerably, from 877 to 962, earning the Danbury chapter the title of Most Improved Chorus in the division in 2003.[9]

However, the Joel Knecht era would not last long. In January 2004, Knecht announced he would step down as director after the May 2004 annual show, in order to "concentrate on his professional studies." Knecht proposed that he might be able to return as director after his graduation in May 2005. The board commented that "his presence will be sorely missed." In his absence, the Board nominated Joe Hudson as the interim director. Joe Hudson has held the Directorship of the Chorus ever since. In reflecting on his tenure in the May 2004 *Hatter Chatter*, Joel Knecht offered the following revealing reflections on his tenure:

> Back in October of 2002, I never would have been able to foresee where the Mad Hatters would be in May of 2004. In that time, we have gone from show to show and contest to contest showing constant improvement. My personal mission when I joined Danbury in October of 2002 was very selfish; I really wanted to direct a chorus. Well I got that chance.[10]

During the same meeting in which Knecht's resignation was announced, the board approved Jim Hopper's application to rejoin the Mad Hatters. A member from 1969 to 1973 who served as secretary of the Chapter who was also a member briefly in 1993–1994, Hopper would prove integral to the chorus early in the twenty-first century.[11] In February 2005, Hopper joined Don Sutherland and Bill Manion as an assistant director to Hudson, a position he retained until 2014.

Hudson was only twenty-one years of age, and still a college student at WCSU, when he took over the direction of the chorus. Fortunately, he not only was the recipient of a top-quality music education at Western, but he was also growing as a director under the tutelage of the experienced assistant directors. In particular, Hudson remembers the patient guidance of Bill Manion as formative for him.[12]

Hudson won over the chorus by making them a part of his extended family. Chorus members from 2004 recall with fondness their most meaningful performance as one from July of that year, in which Hudson asked them to perform the Irving Berlin song "Always" at the Stop and Shop Supermarket in Danbury, where Hudson worked along with his girlfriend, Elizabeth Ehli. At the end of the song, Hudson dropped to one knee and proposed marriage to Ehli, a secondary education major at WCSU.[13] Through integrating the chorus into his life events, Hudson created a kind of paternalistic relationship with its members, who were mostly men in their fifties, sixties, and seventies. The members of the chorus respected his musical knowledge and looked upon him affectionately as a surrogate son (in Bob Bradley's joking words "the son they wished they never had") of whom they were proud and whose legacy they had to protect and nurture. They were motivated to sing for him.

When Hudson graduated from WCSU with a degree in music education in 2006, there happened to be an opening for the choral director at Danbury High School, and he applied. The chorus, which had several members with connections to the high school, called and wrote letters to the administration and staff of Danbury High urging them to hire Joe. The comments are a good bellwether of the chorus's esteem for their director.

One chorus member told the high school: "Hudson knows what greatness sounds like. He also is quick to identify what, in a performance, stands between mediocrity and greatness—and more important, how to explain it to his singers." Another said: "although he insists on high standards, he has an unerring instinct for the right moment to inject humor, self-criticism, or praise that keeps everyone in a top singing mood. He's a hard taskmaster, but his burden is light." A final letter captured the dynamic of the respect for Hudson in the chorus: "Even though he's a twenty-something leading a group of executives, scientists, educators, a doctor, several Ph.D. engineers, and others who are two or three times his age, Joe is a commanding figure, never intimidated and always respected." On August 15, 2006, Hudson walked in to rehearsal and announced that he was "Joseph Hudson, Director of the Danbury Mad Hatters—and Director of the Choral Department at Danbury High School!" The chorus broke out into wild cheers.[14]

On December 29th of that year, Joseph Hudson and Elizabeth Ehli were married in Saint Peter's Church in Danbury, and the Mad Hatters were there, in their black tuxedos and cummerbunds. At the direction of the priest, they began to sing a stirring rendition of the Lord's Prayer that brought tears to Hudson's eyes. After the wedding, he told the chorus:

"You performed at my proposal, and now you're here at my wedding, but I'm sorry, you just can't come along on the honeymoon!"[15]

Every barbershop singing chapter has a foundation built on the connections and friendships of their members. What Joe Hudson managed to do in the early years of his career as Director of the Mad Hatters was to build a close and personal, even familial, relationship with the men under his direction. They wanted him to succeed, and they were willing to work to make the chapter better, as much for him as for themselves.

During his tenure as music director, Joe Hudson has cultivated the "Danbury Sound." Musically, he gives emphasis to the production of good singing through encouraging singers to project no more than six inches in front of them and to develop a freely produced tone that is resonant but also has a forward placement. In the warm-up and craft portion of the rehearsal, Hudson can always be counted on to introduce new exercises that reinforce this thesis. This emphasis has helped the chapter to fix those issues emphasized in the chorus evaluations of the 1990s, eliminating the problem of having individual voices stick out.

Early in Hudson's tenure, in 2005, under the leadership of President Bob Bradley, the chorus was able to move its rehearsals from the Elks Club to the Church of Christ on Clapboard Hill Road in Danbury. In 2004, the Elks had forced the chorus to sign a contract that raised their rent considerably and placed demands on them to do extensive cleaning of the hall after rehearsals. Moreover, the facilities had been disintegrating for quite some time. The Rathskeller Bar, long the focus of informal singing for the chorus, had been closed in the late 1980s due to fire code problems, and the stage area was in a state of disrepair.[16] Fortunately, chapter member and church elder Jim Hopper was able to work out a very reasonable deal for the use of the Church of Christ.

The chorus was motivated by its affection for Hudson to work on improving. This led to competitive success and also to the emergence of new quartets. On May 8, 2004, at the Chorus Contest in Hartford, Connecticut, the Danbury chapter jumped to fourth in the division and won the Small Chorus Championship, singing a set of "Always" and "Fortune in Dreams."[17] Though undoubtedly this achievement reflects the work of Joel Knecht as much as Joe Hudson, it was again an indication to the membership that their work was paying off. Scores continued to improve. In the 2005 districts, the Mad Hatters scored a lackluster 50.7. Yet at the 2006 Division Contest in Berlin, Connecticut, singing "Old Saint Louie" and "You Make Me Feel So Young," they scored a 59.8, with twenty-two men on the risers. By the 2008 contest in Wappinger's Falls, New York, the Mad Hatters were scoring a 62.5—well into the "B" range of choruses. Singing "Over the Rainbow" and "Heart," the Mad Hatters in particular had very high scores (68 and 67) in the singing category, which was both the category Hudson most emphasized and the category in which the chorus had experienced the most trouble previously. The Mad Hatters captured the Best Small Chorus title again that year, as well as the title for most improved. Since that time, the chorus has consistently had scores in the B range. Though they have not found ways to significantly expand their membership or climb into the top echelons of district competition, the Mad Hatters had recovered from the deterioration of the 1990s to become a chorus with a good sound.[18]

2004 also saw the emergence of a long-lasting chapter quartet, Rare Occasion, originally featuring Fred Baran on tenor, Paul Just on lead, Jim Hopper on baritone, and Bill Manion on bass. After Paul Just and Bill Manion moved to Florida, in 2006 and 2009 respectively, they were replaced by Robert Golenbock on lead and Terry Dunkle on bass. Rare Occasion continued performing until 2013.

Around 2010, two new chapter quartets emerged. The song learning methods first implemented by Joel Knecht emphasized the importance of the section leaders acting as a teaching quartet to expedite the learning of songs. As a consequence, the section leaders sang with each other quite frequently, and decided it would be enjoyable to sing together in competition. In a Spanglish wink to the chorus's moniker, they called themselves Loco Fedora. The group featured Joe Hudson on tenor, Robert Golenbock on lead, Jim Hopper on baritone, and Dick Zang on bass. Loco Fedora continued to compete and perform until 2014, and enjoyed considerable success, qualifying for the district competition in 2013.

4.1 *Loco Fedora at Danbury's First Night 2011*

In addition, 2010 brought tenor Tim Kaiser and baritone Wynn Gadkar-Wilcox into the fold of the chorus. That same year, they teamed with lead Danny Anderson and bass Andy Bayer to form Traveling Men. Traveling Men had several different iterations. After Kaiser moved to Oklahoma, he was replaced by Alex Zobler on tenor; when Zobler left the chorus, Daryl Bornstein joined the group on baritone and Gadkar-

Wilcox switched to tenor; when Bornstein left, the group briefly consisted of Andy Bayer on tenor, Danny Anderson on lead, Wynn Gadkar-Wilcox on baritone, and Chuck Kreiger on bass. In 2013, the Traveling Men settled in to the lineup in which it achieved the most success, featuring Art Cilley on tenor, Danny Anderson on lead, Wynn Gadkar-Wilcox on baritone, and Andy Bayer on bass. Traveling Men has enjoyed modest success. They were named the Division's most improved quartet three years in a row, in 2012, 2013, and 2014, and competed in the division contest in 2014 and 2015. In 2016, Art Cilley replaced Gadkar-Wilcox on baritone and the group added a new member, Richard Schoonmaker, on tenor.

In 2015, a new group formed which included two members of the former quartets Loco Fedora and Rare Occasion. The new group, Blue Moon, features Art Cilley on tenor, Robert Golenbock on lead, Jim Hopper on baritone, and Keith Korb on bass. Though still relatively new, Blue Moon has developed a smooth sound that has made them already a favorite on chapter shows and in afterglows.

Finally, Joe Hudson teamed up with the co-directors of the Poughkeepsie Chorus and the director of the Central Connecticut Chorus to

4.2 *Traveling Men*

form the quartet SUREFIRE! in 2013. Featuring Hudson on tenor, Tony Nasto on lead, Garry "Butch" Ashdown on baritone, and John Hadigan on bass, SUREFIRE! won the division championship in 2013 and was a perennial competitor at the top of the district, placing as high as fourth in the district in 2015. They disbanded shortly thereafter.

In the early 1990s, one of the main complaints that led members to leave the chorus was the lack of formal or informal quartetting opportunities. Under the leadership first of Knecht and later Hudson, this problem has clearly been alleviated. Danbury has been blessed with a number of good quartets. These have included both those that focus primarily on being excellent performance and sing-out quartets, such as Real Chemistry, and good competition-focused quartets such as Loco Fedora and Traveling Men.

At the end of 2009, Bob Bradley ended a thirteen-year run as president of the chorus. Much of the success of the chapter in this period can be attributed to him. He righted the ship of the chorus. Upon entering as president in the late 1990s, he first focused on creating a relaxed and fun atmosphere. Bradley, who frequently shows up to rehearsals in neon pink socks and without shoes, could never be accused of taking himself too seriously, and he encouraged the chorus to also not do so. Amazingly, even as the quality of the chorus was still low, Bradley managed to attract and increase membership, with the help of key chapter officers such as Dick Walter and John Bradley and with the musical help of Bill Manion and Don Sutherland, by creating an accepting and fun environment. It was Bradley, as much as anyone, who embraced the concept of the youth movement and who shepherded Joe Hudson into the position as director. When Bradley took over, it was still possible the Mad Hatters would not make it to their golden anniversary. At the end of his tenure, it was clear that the chorus would be in reasonably good shape for some time to come.

In 2010, Danny Anderson replaced Robert Bradley as President of the Chorus. Born in the Gulf Coast area of Alabama, Anderson grew up in the Florida Panhandle. After a long career in sales with the Hallmark Card company, Anderson moved to Danbury, and eventually found himself doing energy work with Efficient Lighting and Maintenance, Inc. in Brookfield, Connecticut. Anderson has focused his presidency, which continues to the present day, on keeping the Mad Hatters in a solid financial position, increasing membership, and making connections between the Mad Hatters and the local community. In his words: "I see this as a service position, where I will enlist the aid of others to help our chapter grow in numbers, strengthen our financial position and expand the community awareness of barbershop music."[19] Though membership has not increased, Anderson has been very successful in maintaining good administration, keeping the organization in an excellent financial position, and increasing the emphasis on sing-outs in the community for the benefit of local retirement homes and charities.

In the 2010s, as Hudson continued to push the envelope in encouraging better singing and contest success for the chorus, cleavages in the chapter began to open. These tensions arose over multiple issues. Under the leadership of long-time Vice President of Music Jim Hopper, and with Hudson's strong influence, the chorus worked to expand its repertoire. It would continue to sing Barbershop tunes, but would expand its music to other genres. During this time, the chorus began to sing classically-oriented arrangements of such songs as "Loch Lomond" and "Shenandoah" and started singing considerably more pop and rock music, such as Queen's 1979 hit "Crazy Little Thing Called Love," a medley of Beach Boys Tunes, and the Jason Mraz song "I'm Yours."

This change in repertoire concerned some long-term members of the chorus, who joined the Barbershop Harmony Society (as SPEBSQSA now calls themselves informally) because it gave them an opportunity to sing great music. Dick Walter, in particular, laments the loss of great repertoire songs such as "Pal of My Cradle Days," "If You Knew Susie," "Little Pal," and "Alexander's Ragtime Band."[20] The chorus was torn between trying a more contemporary repertoire to encourage new and younger membership and maintaining its mission to preserve Barbershop Quartet Singing, as well as preserving the traditions of the Danbury chapter.

Similarly, as Joe Hudson pushed the chorus to improve further, some long-time members became concerned about the excessive rigor of rehearsals. In an effort to spur improvement, around 2012, Hudson, Hopper and the rest of the Music Committee made the decision to spend the vast majority of rehearsal time on the risers, rather than in chairs. This was an effort to enhance concentration and increase the seriousness of rehearsals. In 2015, the chapter meeting time was changed from 7:30 to 7:15 on Tuesdays to encourage more singing. Gradually, certain fun activities of the chapter, such as step-out quartetting, tag time, member biographical introductions, and informal quartetting work, were reduced or eliminated. While this move helped to reset the focus of the chorus, some members felt that it eliminated the fun of rehearsals.

In addition, the Mad Hatters began to intensify their program of coaching. Since 2010, the main coach of the Mad Hatters has been Joe Hunter, the former director of the Big Apple Chorus in New York. He has helped the chorus improve in all categories, but particularly in its

4.3 *SUREFIRE!*

ability to interpret a song and deliver a heartfelt presentation. The chorus has responded to Hunter's winning personality, good humor, and cunning intellect, and his suggestions have helped the chorus improve not only in presentation but also in music.

The second main coach during this period was Daryl Bornstein, who was also a member of the chapter between 2011 and 2014. Bornstein came to the chapter with an impressive musical pedigree and considerable experience with barbershop. Bornstein, who is originally from Syracuse, New York, graduated with a BA in Music from Dartmouth College and embarked on a musical career that took him to being the road manager for Lou Reed and the personal assistant to Leonard Bernstein. Meanwhile, he acquired skills as a sound designer and engineer, and performed that work at a number of important venues on Broadway and elsewhere.[21]

In the course of this work, in the late 1990s, Bornstein became the sound engineer for the Barbershop Harmony Society's international contests, a job he performed for several years; during that time, he acquired an interest in barbershop singing. Upon visiting the chapter in 2011, he immediately impressed the chorus with his voice and knowledge, though they were unaware of his background in music. After the rehearsal, Dick Zang wrote to the Music Committee with a list of Bornstein's credits, noting that "I think he can handle our sound needs and he's got a great voice. Let's hope he joins up."[22]

Between 2012 and 2014, Bornstein was very active as an informal coach and adviser to Director Joe Hudson, and he continues to coach the chorus on occasion. He was particularly significant as a coach in late 2013 and early 2014. His coaching style complemented Hudson's directing style. They could, and did, play "good cop/bad cop." Hudson's deep and enduring friendship with nearly everyone on the risers evokes deep affection and loyalty from the members of the chapter, which is a rare and irreplaceable quality for a director to have. On the other hand, this leadership quality, which is produced by Hudson's warmth and non-confrontational demeanor, inhibits his ability to give the chapter members the direct criticism they sometimes need. Moreover, the love and respect the chorus members feel for their director impedes their ability to have frank conversations in which they might express concerns about individual aspects of his leadership. Bornstein, by contrast, is direct and critical to a fault. For sensitive chapter members, his bluntness could occasionally rise to the level of a counterproductive callousness.

These men, with two diametrically opposed personalities, must not have found working with each other very easy; on the other hand, for the chorus, the combination of the two provided the right balance between positive reinforcement and constructive criticism. It is no accident that the Mad Hatters achieved their greatest success at the March 2014 division contest, where the Mad Hatters reached an average score of 65.8 and won both the division's small chorus championship and most improved chorus, and coming in second overall in the division competition, a result not seen since the early 1980s.

However, the hard-driving work of the Mad Hatters in 2013 and 2014 produced some resistance from members of the chapter who preferred more socially oriented chapter meetings. This led to a perennial debate about whether the chorus is a "competition" chorus (one that focuses on success in division, district, or international competitions), a "performance chorus" (one that focuses on performing for the community) or a "social chorus" (one that focuses on barbershop singing as a fun activity and concentrates on developing the chapter meetings as a time for socializing). This debate goes back to at least 2010.[23] In fact, the chapter has had a consistent answer to this question for some time, about which there seems be considerable agreement on the Board of Directors: the chorus is, and always has been, chiefly a performance chorus that frequently also competes and also tries to emphasize fun and camaraderie at chapter meetings.

The disagreement about the mission of the chorus is really about the degree to which each of these aspects should be emphasized. President Danny Anderson, Secretary Robert Golenbock, and Vice President for

Music Wynn Gadkar-Wilcox generally argue for more emphasis to be placed on competitions. Member at large and long-time former VP of Music and Assistant Director Jim Hopper, as well as treasurer Dickson DeMarche, favor an emphasis on performance and sing-outs. Long-time member Dick Walter favors placing more emphasis on fun and social activities in the chorus.

4.4 *Real Chemistry*

From 2014 to the present, the chorus has tried to respond to all of these voices by attempting to accommodate all perspectives. The result, however, appears to be that rather than succeeding in all three aspects of the chapter's activity, the Mad Hatters gradually failing to do any of the three as well as they did previously. The chapter has lost focus while trying to do too much at the same time. Contest scores are slowly slipping;

at the 2016 division contest, the chorus, singing "It's a Brand New Day" and "May I Never Love Again," slipped to an average of 61.1 and scored second-to-last in the district. In its effort to be all-of-the-above (excelling at competition and sing-outs while simultaneously having entertaining chapter meetings), the chorus risks creating an organization that does none-of-the-above. The chorus's position seems most analogous to the position of the chorus in 1985. Despite considerable recent success, a talented Music Director to whom the chorus is loyal, and a dedicated and stable membership, the chorus seems on the path to a slow and inexorable decline due to a lack of focus and commitment and an inability to rally around new and fresh ideas.

Under Tony Grosz, the Mad Hatter Chorus showed that it was indeed possible to be an "all-of-the-above" chorus. Grosz galvanized the chorus with new ideas that would simultaneously satisfy all three aspects of the life of a chapter: competition success, performance opportunities in the community, and great social events for the chapter. Grosz emphasized that every member of the chapter should be in a quartet. He organized informal competitions within the chorus, excited the chorus with daring arrangements of new music, helped organize informal competitions between chapters with the Danbury Cup, and helped bring the community to the chorus while simultaneously promoting entertainment and fun with the show-glows. The current chorus could learn a great deal from the steps that led to the (unfortunately evanescent) explosion of the chorus's size to nearly 100 members in the mid-1970s.

The current chorus decided to forego the 2016 District contest to focus on improving its musical abilities. Perhaps that will give it time to organize and implement daring new ideas such as those implemented by the chorus of forty years ago. The chorus could successfully integrate all aspects of its mission. Recent history, however, may not give much reason to hope that this can be done. In 2012, the chorus skipped the district contest over a concern that there might not have been sufficient lead singers and because of a desire to spend more time focusing on craft. The result was that at the 2013 division contest, the chorus scored on average nearly three points lower than they had in the previous year.

Nor does it appear likely that the chorus will improve through expanding its membership. The Barbershop Harmony Society's magazine, *The Harmonizer*, frequently publishes success stories recounting how innovative chapters have adopted strategies to rapidly increase membership. One recent story discusses the success of a new "fun" chapter in San Antonio.[24] This article highlights the strategies for which the leadership of this organization should be given credit. However, just as important is that San Antonio had the requisite demographic trends to make such transformations possible. For example, San Antonio is sixth in the nation in population growth and its growth has been fueled by an economic expansion that has produced jobs in technology and health care and has brought white-collar upper-middle class workers with free time and disposable income to the city.[25] The same is not the case in western Connecticut, where white-collar employers in the health care and technology industries, such as General Electric and Aetna, have left or are threatening to leave the region.[26] Western Connecticut is experiencing the inverse of the boom in white-collar jobs that helped fuel the expansion of the Danbury chapter in the 1960s and 1970s.

Now more than ever, any potential improvements in the quality of the chorus, and the expansion of membership that would come from such improvements, can only be obtained if the chapter leadership has the courage to take bold and audacious steps. The chorus needs to make moves that are a substantial departure from the status quo. Only time will tell whether the chapter is ready to make such changes.

However, the Mad Hatters will not descend into the existential crisis in which it found itself in the early 1990s. The Danbury chapter today consists of a very tight-knit group of men who respect one another. It is run by an extremely capable Board of Directors and a talented Music Director. It is financially stable. Its membership, while not expanding, is unlikely to decline.

One of the very few songs that the Danbury chapter has sung at some point in every decade from its inception in the 1960s to the present day is "On the Sunny Side of the Street," composed by Jimmy McHugh in 1930 with words by Dorothy Fields. It is appropriate that this is the chorus's most enduring song. From its origins, the chapter has been known for its hospitality, its sense of *joie de vivre*, and the closeness of its membership. It is a sunny chapter, with a positive outlook, whose members deeply enjoy each other's company.

One can see a glimpse of the madcap antics of Joe Talarico in the whimsical tendency of *Hatter Chatter* editor John Bradley to insert fake song titles, such as "I Gave Her My Heart and a Diamond and She Clubbed Me with a Spade" or "She Got the Gold Mine (I Got the Shaft)" into the official listing of the chorus's repertoire.[27] One sees the spirit of the 1960s Nutmegger quartet, who once went to the Bronx Zoo to serenade an octopus to the tune of "How Many Arms Have Held You," in the screwball minutes from secretary Robert Golenbock (also humorously edited by John Bradley), which frequently list such phantom guests at the board meetings as Sting, Colin Powell, or Mister Ed.[28] It is this spirit that makes the Danbury chapter special, and it is this sunny and positive attitude that will animate the chapter for another fifty years to come and beyond.

Notes

1 "Voices in Harmony," (2001 Annual Show Program), 1998–2007 files, Chorus Archive.

2 Minutes of Board of Directors, Danbury Chapter, May 2, 2002.

3 *Ibid.*

4 Minutes of Board of Directors, Danbury Chapter, Nov 7, 2002.

5 Minutes of Music and Performance Committee, Danbury Chapter, January 5, 2003.

6 Joseph Hudson, personal interview, May 5, 2016.

7 Joel R. Knecht, "Rehearsal Guidelines," (2003), 1998–2007 files, Chorus Archive.

8 Joel R. Knecht, "Chapter Novice Quartet Proposal (2003), 1998–2007 files, Chorus Archive.

9 Official Scoring Summary, NED, Yankee Division, Chorus Finals, Saratoga Springs, NY, April 5, 2003. Retrieved May 6, 2016. http://www.nedistrict.org/scores.

10 Joel R. Knecht, "Thanks for Everything," *Hatter Chatter* 10:5 (May 2004):1.

11 Minutes of Board of Directors, Danbury Chapter, Jan 6, 2004.

12 Joseph Hudson, personal interview, May 5, 2016.

13 "Stop and Pop the Question," *The News-Times* (July 19, 2004). Retrieved May 6, 2016. http://www.newstimes.com/news/article/Stop-and-pop-the-question-61444.php.

14 Terry Dunkle, "Joseph P. Hudson, Music Director," (2013) The Mad Hatter Chorus. Retrieved May 6, 2016. http://madhatterchorus.org/director.

15 *Ibid.*

16 Dick Zang, personal interview, Feb 16, 2016.

17 Official Scoring Summary, NED, Yankee Division, Chorus Finals, West Hartford, Connecticut, May 8, 2004. Retrieved May 6, 2016. http://www.nedistrict.org/scores/.

18 Official Scoring Summaries, NED, Yankee Division, Chorus Finals, 2006 and 2008. Retrieved May 6, 2016. http://www.nedistrict.org/scores/.

19 "Meet Our New President," *Hatter Chatter* 17:1 (Jan 2010):4.

20 Dick Walter, personal interview, February 21, 2016.

21 "Daryl Bornstein: Audio Coach," *Mad Hatter Chorus*. Retrieved May 6, 2016. http://madhatterchorus.org/node/58.

22 Dick Zang, email to the Music Committee, November 3, 2011.

23 See Robert Golenbock's letter to Editors of the Hatter Chatter, *Hatter Chatter* 17:10 (October 2010):4.

24 "Just Having Fun," *The Harmonizer* (March/April 2016):22–24.

25 Vianna Davila, "San Antonio Area is Number Six in Population Growth in the U.S.," *San Antonio Express-News* (March 24, 2016), retrieved May 6, 2016, http://www.expressnews.com/news/local/article/San-Antonio-area-is-No-6-inpopulation-growth-in-7030115.php; Robert Rivard, "Forecast, San Antonio Economy to Remain Sunny," *The Rivard Report* (March 20, 2015), retrieved May 6, 2016, http://therivardreport.com/forecast-san-antonio-economy-toremain-sunny/.

26 Steven Singer, "AETNA says that Kentucky is the only place where it's made a real estate commitment," *Hartford Courant* (February 1, 2016), retrieved May 6, 2016, http://www.courant.com/business/connecticut-insurance/hc-aetnaleaving-hartford-20160201-story.html; Steven Singer, "General Electric Moving Headquarters to Boston," *Hartford Courant* (January 13, 2016), retrieved May 6, 2016, http://www.courant.com/business/hc-boston-ge-moving-20160113-story.html.

27 "Current Mad Hatter Repertoire," *Hatter Chatter* 23:2 (March 2016):9; "Current Mad Hatter Repertoire," *Hatter Chatter* 23:3 (April 2016):9.

28 Royce, "No Message, Just Pleasure," "Board of Directors Meeting," *Hatter Chatter* 23:2 (March 2016):6; "Board of Directors Meeting," *Hatter Chatter* 23:3 (April 2016):6.

Epilogue

The bulk of this book was completed in April 2016, so that rough copies could be distributed to several former members of the Mad Hatters who traveled long distances to join the chorus on its fiftieth anniversary show, "It's a Brand New Day," which was held on May 7, 2016. While it is difficult for a historian to reflect on events so close to the present, and perhaps impossible to determine what their significance will turn out to be, so much of importance has occurred since that time that it seems necessary to recount these events.

Inspired in part by reading a draft of this history, Vice President of Membership Terry Dunkle crafted an ambitious plan for the chorus focused on membership growth. Dunkle contacted Executive Vice President of the Chapter Andy Bayer and Vice President of Music Wynn Gadkar-Wilcox for advice about his plan. Together, the three met several times in the summer and fall of 2016. Under Dunkle's leadership, they premiered a draft of a bold membership plan at a supplemental board meeting in November 2016. The plan set a goal of reaching 100 members by 2021. It proposed that there were three major avenues for increasing membership: rapidly improving singing quality, more effectively reaching out to potential singers in the area, and seeking out both a new rehearsal venue and new places in the community at which to sing.[1]

Supporting Dunkle's daring vision would require effort, energy, and money from the chorus and its members. The plan for improving singing quality involved setting clear goals, implementing more quartet singing, exponentially increasing the coaching budget for the chorus, offering chorus members private singing lessons partially paid through chorus funds, and supporting a visiting "artist in residence." To improve outreach, Dunkle and his team proposed encouraging dual members from nearby chapters, inviting previous attendees and members back into the fold, and most importantly, advertising and marketing aimed at attracting the younger generation as well as an increasing demographic within Danbury: the Spanish and Portuguese-speaking resident. Dunkle observed that while Danbury's median age was thirty-five and just over half of the city is white, the Mad Hatters had a median age of sixty-five and the chorus appeared to be entirely white.[2] He suggested aggressively advertising in the region's non-English newspapers, introducing the Mad Hatters to the local Portuguese Cultural Center and other similar centers in the area, and expanding our repertoire to appeal to the diverse and younger population of Danbury. Dunkle linked the prospect of attracting a more diverse crowd to the chorus's lack of visibility. He and his team urged the chorus to sing at new venues, such as at open mic nights, block-party barbeques, barbershops, and flash mobs, and to seek a permanent new rehearsal location nearer to the city center.[3] The Board gave Dunkle and his team provisional acceptance of their plan at their retreat in January 2017 pending the presentation of a viable five-year business model and evidence of buy-in from the chorus membership.[4]

By the fall of 2016, the Music Committee independently began approving several music-related ideas in Dunkle's plan. They adopted clear goals to be achieved by the Division contest in 2017. The chorus would focus on a series of bimonthly skills known as the "Six S's Plan": smile, stay on top of the pitch, sing through the phrase, stop singing so loudly, sound like a unit, and stay focused. The goals that these skills would help achieve were to have twenty-five men on the risers at the Division Convention at Lake George, New York, in May 2017, and to win the chorus's plateau at that competition. In furtherance of these goals, the Music

Committee also committed to arranging all chorus singers in informal chapter quartets, organizing chorus retreats, and booking coaching from local standouts Steve Delehanty and Joe Hunter.[5]

In addition, in late 2016, dual members buoyed the ranks of the Mad Hatters. Jordan Kugler, the Vice President of Music with the Bridgeport Chapter, suggested in an interchapter meeting held in Danbury in the summer of 2016 that several of his chapter members were interested in competing and might join Danbury as dual members in order to sing in chorus contests. After a plan for this collaboration was agreed to by both chapters, Kugler, along with Bridgeport's President David Hunter, tenors Russ Lang and Vic Lembo, basses Scott Poarch and Steve Fians, and baritone Bill McDonald, who had been a member of the Mad Hatters during the glory years of the 1970s and 1980s, joined the group. These new dual members were among Bridgeport's best singers. Kugler, Lembo, Hunter, and Poarch together made up Take 4, a quartet that had won the division championship in 2016. In 2017, the Mad Hatters gained two more dual members: Nick LoRusso of the Waterbury/Derby chapter and Bob Serrano from the Westchester chapter.

Bolstered by the new music plan and the new singers, the Mad Hatters achieved success at the 2017 Division competition. With twenty-eight men on the risers, singing "For All We Know" and "After You've Gone," they scored an average of 68.8, up more than seven points from the previous year, and they were named the Most Improved Chorus. While they did not win their plateau, their total score of 825 was only two points behind the plateau winner Central Connecticut, and only four points behind the Division Champions from Manchester, Connecticut.

Despite this musical success, the chorus was divided over the implementation of the growth plan. While the Board had given it tentative approval, President Danny Anderson, Member-at-Large Jim Hopper, and Treasurer Dickson DeMarche were all concerned about the large budget that Dunkle and his team were proposing. They worried whether the chorus membership could be counted on to do the additional fundraising work that would be required to support the tens of thousands of dollars of additional spending being proposed.[6] In May 2017, Dunkle presented the chorus with the final plan, including a detailed explanation of the additional time each chorus member would be expected to spend executing the plan. He then distributed an anonymous survey to members, asking if they supported it, and if they were willing to devote an extra hour per week to helping their chorus grow. While the overwhelming majority of the chorus supported the growth plan, one-third of the members indicated that they would not be willing to put in the extra time necessary to implement it. Given these data, Dunkle decided that the growth plan could not continue to be implemented as he envisioned, and would need to be scaled back.[7]

Subsequent to that decision, Dunkle decided to take a "sabbatical" from the chorus. Though he cited writing his book and focusing on his business as the reason for his hiatus, perhaps the lack of a clearer mandate for his plan may have factored into his decision.[8] Dunkle's extended absence meant that much of the impetus for continuing the positive energy he had created fell to Executive Vice President Andy Bayer, the person with the organizational wherewithal to keep the chorus moving forward toward musical and membership growth. To the extent that the Mad Hatter's unquestionable improvements were due to the implementation of the growth plan, Andy Bayer is most responsible for that success. Unfortunately, in October 2017, tensions between Bayer and President Danny Anderson were brought to the fore when Anderson publicly criticized what he perceived as Bayer's intrusiveness in chorus affairs, prompting Bayer to step down from his administrative positions as Executive Vice President, Membership co-chair, and Uniform Chair. The resignations of Dunkle and Bayer have left an administrative vacuum that threatens to retard the forward momentum of the chorus.

Despite these challenges, however, the Mad Hatters are experiencing a crescendo of musical improvement. In 2017, inspired by the growth plan, the Music Committee adopted a goal of having "A Chorus of Musicians" by 2018. This meant that the committee envisioned a future chorus that would be skilled at sight-singing and reading music and committed to working at making themselves much better singers. To achieve this, in the summer of 2017, the Mad Hatters devoted rehearsal time to music literacy through a series of lessons taught by Assistant Director Scott Colman. Additionally, the chorus's coffers subsidized a series of individual music lessons, followed by lessons in quartets, with the well-known *bel canto* voice instructor and coach Debra Lynn. The music team also booked a series of coaching sessions with Joe Hunter. The rapidly improving sound of the chorus is a testament to the fruit these approaches are bearing.

A year after the fiftieth anniversary of the chorus, the Mad Hatters are on a path toward musical improvement and membership growth. It is too early to say whether the chorus will stay on that path, or take any number of perilous detours. Substantial change is difficult, and will always bring with it some level of animosity and strife. Yet the friendships and loyalty built over decades will prevent the men of the chorus from being torn asunder; they will remain, well into the future, the same slightly irreverent bunch that they were fifty years ago.

Notes

1 Terry Dunkle, "Mad Hatter Chorus: Let's Grow! Board of Directors Presentation, November 29, 2016," Mad Hatter Chorus Archives; Robert Golenbock, "2017 Super Extraordinary Executive Session Retreat, Danbury Mad Hatter Chorus Board of Directors," *Hatter Chatter* 24:1 (Spring Training 2017):7–8.

2 Dunkle, "Let's Grow!"

3 "Mad Hatters Eye Five-Year Growth Campaign," *Hatter Chatter* 24:1 (Spring Training 2017):1–2.

4 *Ibid.*, 1.

5 Wynn Gadkar-Wilcox, "Music Committee Notes," *Hatter Chatter* 23:5 (Early Summer 2016):6.

6 Golenbock, "2017 Super Extraordinary Executive Session Retreat," 7.

7 Terry Dunkle, email to Wynn Gadkar-Wilcox and Andy Bayer, May 17, 2017, in possession of author.

8 Danny Anderson, "President's Podium," *Hatter Chatter* 24:3 (Labor Day 2017):3.

Selected Bibliography

Archives
Truman Warner Collection, Western Connecticut State University Archives, Danbury, CT.
Mad Hatter Chorus Archives, Danbury, CT.

Interviews
Bob Connolley, April 20, 2016.
Jack Cramer (via email), August 13, 2016.
Anton Grosz, May 2, 2016.
Jim Hopper, March 10, 2016.
Joseph Hudson, May 5, 2016.
Bill Manion, March 17, 2016 and May 2, 2016.
Bob Stewart (via email), August 16, 2016.
Dick Walter, February 21, 2016.
Dick Zang, February 16, 2016 and May 3, 2016.

Newspapers and Periodicals
Clio: WCSU History Journal, Danbury, CT.
Connecticut Post (formerly the Bridgeport Post), Bridgeport, CT.
Hartford Courant, Hartford, CT.

Harmonizer, Kenosha, WI and Nashville, TN.
Hatter Chatter, Danbury, CT.
The Hour, Norwalk, CT.
Journal-Advertiser, Danbury, CT.
Monroe Courier, Monroe, CT.
News-Times (formerly The Danbury News-Times), Danbury, CT.
Nor'easter: The Voice of NED Barbershopper, Keene, NH.
San Antonio Express News, San Antonio, TX.

Websites

Barbershop Harmony Society, accessed October 19, 2017, http://barbershop.org.

Carolinas District: Barbershop Harmony Society, accessed October 19, 2017, http://www.carolinasdistrict.org.

Mad Hatter Chorus, accessed October 19, 2017. http://madhatterchorus.org.

Northeastern District: Barbershop Harmony Society, accessed October 19, 2017, nedistrict.org.

The Rivard Report, accessed October 19, 2017. http://www.therivardreport.com.

Other Published Sources

Averill, Gage. *Four Parts, No Waiting: A Social History of American Barbershop Harmony*. New York: Oxford University Press, 2003.

Coltrane, Scott. *Family Man: Fatherhood, Housework, and Gender Equality*. New York: Oxford University Press, 1997.

Devlin, William E., and Herbert F. Janick, *Danbury's Third Century: From Urban Status to Tri-Centennial*. Danbury, CT: Western Connecticut State University, 2013.

Eckerman, Ingrid. *The Bhopal Saga: Causes and Consequences of the World's Largest Industrial Disaster*. Hyderabad, India: Universities Press, 2005.

Fischer, Claude S. *Still Connected: Family and Friends in America since 1970*. New York: Russell Sage Foundation, 2011.

Freeman, Gary. *The Bootleg Guide: Classic Bootlegs of the 1960s and 1970s*. Lanham, MD: Scarecrow Press, 2003.

Grosz, Anton. *Letters to a Dying Friend: Helping Those You Love Make a Conscious Transition*. Wheaton, IL: Thosophical Publishing House, 1989.

Mejia, Rafael, and Priscilla Canny, Ph.D. *Immigration in Connecticut: A Growing Opportunity*. New Haven: CT Kids Link, 2007.

Mook, Richard. "Barbershop," in John Shepherd, David Horn (eds.), *Popular Music of the World, Volume 8*. London: A and C Black, 2008.

Putnam, Robert D. *Bowling Alone: The Collapse and Revival of American Community*. New York: Simon and Schuster, 2001.

Sembor, Edward C. *An Introduction to Connecticut State and Local Government*. Lanham, MD: University Press of America, 2003.

Stebbins, Robert A. *The Barbershop Singer: Inside the Social World of a Musical Hobby*. Toronto: University of Toronto Press, 1996.

Index

A & W Root Beer, 4
A Chorus of Musicians, 114–115
Adventurers, 20
Aetna, 107
Ahearn, John, 20, 34, 36
alcohol, 8, 53
Allen, Bob, 56
Anderson, Danny, 98, 99, 100–101, 104, 113, 114
Angeli, Larry, 49, 50
Ashdown, Butch, 100
Auditions for Admissions Program, 33

backyard singouts, 8, 10, 21–22, 54, 59, 77
Baran, Fred, 97
barbershop conventions and contests
  Division contests, 6, 10, 15, 16, 19, 20, 30, 42, 43, 46, 47, 48, 50, 53, 54, 56, 59, 61, 62, 63, 64, 80, 81, 83, 86, 92, 93, 97, 99, 100, 104, 106, 107, 109, 112, 113
  Northeastern District Conventions, 6, 10, 15, 16, 20, 21, 30, 32, 33, 35, 37, 38, 41, 42, 43, 46, 48, 50, 56, 59, 61, 62, 63, 83, 85, 97, 98, 100, 104, 106
Barbershop Harmony Society 1, 4, 6, 10–11, 14, 20, 22, 42, 58, 61, 64, 73–74
  charter, 1
  educational events, 61
  headquarters, 4
  letter of condolence for Joe Talarico, 78

membership trends, 10–11, 29, 73–74
operating standards, 42
Protention program, 56
Bardo Thodol, 45
Bartley, Bob, 76–79, 82, 84, 86
Bayer, Andy, 98, 99, 111, 114
Beckner, Dick, 4, 49
Bhopal disaster, 64
Binder, Carl, 80
Blue Moon, 99
Bonanducci, Rocco, 82
Bornstein, Daryl, 98 103
Boston Common, 20, 52
Bradley, Bob, 86, 91, 93, 95, 96, 100
Bradley, Jim, 49
Bradley, John, 86, 93, 100, 108
Bristol, Dick, 41, 43, 44
Brotherhood, 15, 38, 67
Buck, Gene, 38, 50
Buddhism, 45
Burns, Art, 15
Bridgeport Chapter, 4, 6–8, 12, 15, 24, 113
Buzaid, Emile, 7

Carlson, Len, 34, 38, 49, 50, 55, 77
Cash, O.C., 1
Central Connecticut Chapter, 99, 113
Church of Christ, Danbury, 96
Cilley, Art, 99
Coastal Chordsmen. *See* Bridgeport Chorus
Cohen, Mike, 79–80
Cold Water Flat, 50
Colman, Scott, 115

Coltrane, Scott, 11
Connecticut Chord Company, 36, 38
Connecticut Wailers, 80
Connolley, Bob, 43, 44–45, 80, 88
Conti, Robert, 4
Cooley, Bill, 39
Coughlin, Clark, 6, 38
counterculture, 3
Craig, Renee, 54, 58, 62
Cramer, Jack, 30, 34, 43, 44, 54, 58, 60
class. *See* social class

D'Aureli, Augie, 93
Danbury Association to Advance the Handicapped and Retarded, 14
Danbury, city of, 2, 29–30
  Clapboard Ridge Road, 4, 96
  ethnic diversity in, 74–75
  Main Street, 2, 7, 9, 43–44, 74
  residents of Cambodian origin, 75
  residents of Portuguese or Brazilian origin, 74, 112
  South Street, 1, 37
  Spanish-speaking residents, 75, 112
Danbury Cup, 36, 64, 106
Danbury Fair Mall, 74
Danbury High School, 3–4, 12, 15, 38, 50, 61, 91, 95
Danbury Motor Inn, 4, 6, 8, 9, 53
Danbury Quartet Challenge Cup. *See* Danbury Cup
Danbury Sound, 96
Dardis, Tom, 15, 22
DaSilva, Joseph, 74
Deane, Jack, 38
Delehanty, Steve, 113
DeMarche, Dickson, 105, 113
Derby Chapter. *See* Waterbury-Derby Chapter
Donatelli, Pete, 38, 45
Doors, the, 3
Duda, Dan, 49, 75, 76, 78, 79, 82
Dunkle, Terry, 97, 111–114
drinking, 10, 53–54

Ehli, Elizabeth. *See* Liz Hudson
Elks Club. *See* Elks Hall
Elks Hall, 7, 8, 9, 10, 12, 30, 33, 52–53, 61, 83, 96
Ellenberger, Dick, 36, 62
Elm City Chorus. *See* New Haven Chapter

Federal Correctional Institute, Danbury, 39
Ferrito, Frank, 53, 54
Fians, Steve, 113
Film Nights, 33–34
Final Decision, 36
Firmender, Ed, 1, 4, 34
Firmender, Craig, 34
Finch, Gordon, 49
Fisk, Chuck, 6
Foley, Jack, 38, 44, 55
Four Statesmen, 6, 12
Four-N-Aires, 38
Four-Tune-Tellers, 14
Fox, Don, 84
fraternal orders, 2, 11, 75

Gadkar-Wilcox, Wynn, 98, 99, 105, 111
General Electric, 107
Gielow, Fred, 38
"Girl" package, 52
Gleissner, Bill, 83
Golden, Frank, 49, 55
Golenbock, Robert, 97, 99, 104, 108
Grandma's Boys, 20,
Great Eastern Union Singing Telegram Company, 50
Griffin, Dan, 93
Grosz, Tony, 12, 15, 20, 22, 30, 32, 35–36, 38, 40–46, 63–65, 106

Hadigan, John, 100
Harmo-Nuts, 14
Hartford County Jail, 38
Harmony University, 56
Harvey, Ed, 49, 84
hat-making, 2
Hess, Dick, 20, 50
Homesteaders, 15
hoopla committee. *See* Ladies' Auxiliary
Hopper, Jim, 16, 84, 94, 96, 97, 98, 101, 105, 113

INDEX

Horhota, Steve, 86, 93
Housatonic-Derby Chapter. *See* Waterbury-Derby Chapter
Hudson, Joe, 92–97, 99, 100, 101, 102, 103
Hudson, Liz, 94–95
Hunter, David, 113
Hunter, Joe, 102, 103, 113, 115

Immaculate High School (Danbury, CT), 36
Interstate 84, 2, 45
Interstate 684, 2

James, Bill, 24–25, 32
Jimenez, Patty, 91
Jones, Fritz, 15
Just, Paul, 97

Kaiser, Tim, 98
Kearney, Bill, 4
Keenan, Bill, 55
Keith, Ron, 93
Kennedy, Paul, 59, 62
King, George, 56, 84
Knecht, Joel, 87, 91–94, 97, 100
Kolp, Hal, 56
Korb, Keith, 99
Kovacs, James, 4
Kreiger, Chuck, 93, 109
Krieger, Don, 15
Kugler, Jordan, 113

LaBosco, John, 49, 63, 64, 75, 78, 80
Ladies' Auxiliary, 22, 33, 52, 76
Lake Placid, 30, 35, 48, 54, 63
Last Call, 36, 38
Lavender Hill Mob, 20, 22, 32, 34, 35, 36, 38
Leety, Bob, 80
Lembo, Vic, 113
Lesperance, Andre, 76
Light, Aubrey, 15
Loco Fedora, 97, 98, 99, 100
Logan, John, 84
LoRusso, Nick, 113
Lynn, Debra, 115

Macgregor, Jack, 6, 12
Mad Hatter Chorus
  Board of Directors, 1, 8, 12, 16, 39, 60–61, 107
Mad Hatter Rascals, 38, 77
Maino, Al, 6
May, Ona, 20
male bonding, 2, 10–11
Manchester Chapter, 50, 62, 113
Manion, Bill, 9, 12–14, 16, 20–21, 30–32, 38, 42, 49, 54, 56, 58, 63, 67, 78, 83–84, 86–87, 91–92, 94, 97, 100
manufacturing, 29, 74
Marino, Victor, 4
Martino, John, 4
McCarthy, Tom, 86
McDonald, Bill, 113
McFarlane, Mike, 55
Meade, Ron, 38
Meriden Chapter, 6, 16, 62
Merolle, Mario, 38, 44, 49
Merkling, Frank, 29–30
Millett, Joe, 6
Mook, Richard, 73
Music Man, 2
Myers, Mike, 37, 38

Nashua, New Hampshire Chapter, 36, 46, 52
Nasto, Tony, 100
New Deal, 1
New Fairfield High School, 12, 50
New Haven Chapter, 6, 14, 24
New London Chapter, 16, 50, 85
New York City, 2, 29, 32, 69
New York State, 10, 20, 36, 45, 48, 86, 97, 102, 103, 112
News-Times (Danbury, CT), 3, 14, 29, 74
Newyorkers chorus. *See* Poughkeepsie Chapter
Noblemen, 15
Noonan, John, 84
Northeastern District (of the Barbershop Harmony Society), 6, 9, 14, 35
nostalgia, 11
Note-Wits, 15–16, 61
Noto, Michael, 6, 12
Nutmeg Heritage, 56, 59
Nutmeggers, 12, 14, 15, 98

Octet. *See* Mad Hatter Rascals
Otten, Gerry, 84
Over the Hill Mob, 36

package shows, 14–15, 35, 53
Penthouse Four, 20, 35
Perkins, John, 41
Persuaders, 6, 9, 12, 25
Pittsfield Chapter, 18, 53
Plumb, Steve, 15, 32, 54, 61
Poarch, Scott, 113
Pollitt, Wes, 83–84
Poughkeepsie Chapter, 6, 8, 13–15, 20, 30, 32, 34–35, 37, 38, 45, 54
Protention Program, 20, 56

qualifications, 19, 40, 56

race riots, 3
Random Sample, 36, 38
Rare Occasion, 97, 99
Rathskeller Bar, 10, 30, 51, 53, 83, 96
Real Chemistry, 93, 100
Right Blend, 80–81
Ringmaster's Chorus. *See* Bridgeport Chapter
RISE (Rapid Improvement in Singing Excellence) Program, 60, 61
Roberts, Art, 93
Rocket Tones, 12, 14
Rogues Four, 6
Roosevelt, Franklin D., 1
Rosendahl, Burt, 49
"Rosie" set, 29, 54
Royce, Bob, 32
Royce, Lynne, 14, 15
Rushton, Stan, 55
Ryder, Ed, 9

Saint Gregory the Great Church, 50
Saint Peter's Church, 14, 95
San Antonio, 103
San Francisco, 41, 45
Saratoga Springs Chapter, 38
Schetler, Ray, 16
Schoonmaker, Richard, 93, 99

Schwerdt, George, 79–80, 83
Sea Notes. *See* New London Chapter
Serrano, Bob, 113
Seymore, Hank, 15
show glows, 34, 84–85, 106
Slack, Bruce, 15
social activities, 3, 10, 73, 105, 106
social change, 14, 75
social class, 10, 30, 74, 75, 107
Society for the Preservation and Encouragement of Barbershop Quartet Singing in America (SPEBSQSA). *See* Barbershop Harmony Society
Soundsmen, 12
Speglevin, Joe, 4
Spenard, Jack, 55
Still River flood of 1955, 2
Smith, Bob, 38
Smith, Don, 86
Stanczak, Bob, 49, 77, 78
Stewart, Bob, 38, 43, 44, 49, 50, 55
Summertime, 55
SUREFIRE!, 99–100
Sutherland, Don, 12, 79, 83–84, 86, 92, 94, 100
Sweet Adelines, 16

Talarico, Joe, 4, 22, 38, 59, 77–78, 108
Taylor, Lawrence, 16
Technology industry, 2–3, 29, 74
Tenaglia, John, 49
Thompson, Al, 12
Tibetan Book of the Dead. *See* Bardo Thodol
Torielli, Bob, 81
Traveling Men, 98, 99, 100
Two Plus Two Four, 16
Tyler, Jack, 38
uniforms, 4, 16, 35, 48

Union Carbide, 29, 64
Unlikely Hoods, 14

Valley Chordsmen. *See* Waterbury-Derby Chapter
Van Derzee, Ed, 77

INDEX

Waldron, Ray, 38, 42
Wallick, Bud, 15
Walter, Dick, 86, 93, 100, 101, 105
Waterbury-Derby Chapter, 34, 38, 46, 47, 60, 62, 113
WCSU. *See* Western Connecticut State University
Westchester Chapter, 58, 113
Western Connecticut State University, 91, 92, 94, 95
Williams, Jack, 6, 16, 38, 50
Wixted, Marion, 50
Wixted, Ray, 1, 3, 12, 15, 20, 22, 24, 26, 30, 37, 41–50, 52, 54, 56, 62, 64–65, 78, 80, 85–86
World War II, 2, 49

Yankee Peddlers, 16

Zang, Dick, 32–33, 34, 50, 54, 63, 80, 98, 103
Zerrelly, Pete, 15
Zobler, Alex, 98

design, layout,
and typography
by **H.G. Salome** of
Bristol, Vermont USA

www.metaglyfix.com

www.ingramcontent.com/pod-product-compliance
Lightning Source LLC
Chambersburg PA
CBHW072050290426
44110CB00014B/1629